How to Live
with Your
OLD HOUSE

How to Live with Your OLD HOUSE

Written
and
Illustrated by
JOAN WEBBER

McGraw-Hill Book Company

New York   St. Louis
San Francisco   Hamburg
London   Mexico
Sydney   Toronto

1 2 3 4 5 6 7 8 9 0 M U M U 8 7 6 5 4 3 2 1

LIBRARY OF CONGRESS CATALOGING IN PUBLICATION DATA

Webber, Joan, 1933–
How to Live with Your Old House
1. Dwellings—Maintenance and repair.   I. Title.
TH4817.W4   643'.7   80-26987
ISBN 0-07-068791-9

Book design by Roberta Rezk.

This book is dedicated to
Elizabeth, John and George.

They may feel it risky to immortalize our
home and life-style, but without my children,
there would have been no large and erratic
old house and no story to tell.

Contents

"relax"

Introduction

As the owner of an old house, it came to me one day that since my family and I have developed a reasonably decent way of life under its constantly demanding conditions, I would be selfish not to pass on a few practical ideas to others. My first and most profoundly heartfelt message is, relax, everything is going to be all right. Like any experience that is uncertain at first, but familiar in no time, life in an old house quickly becomes "old shoe," if you remain calm and philosophical.

How old is an old house? When I lived in California, we bought a Spanish-style home in a heavily populated neighborhood in Palo Alto. Ours was the first house to be built on the street and when new, it was surrounded by a flourishing walnut grove. That house, built in 1927, was old by California standards. By Midwestern measure, it was not so aged, and an Easterner seeking an old house would not bother to look at it.

As a child in New England, I grew up in a cavernous place that my grandparents built in 1900. My mother longed to live in an *old* house and scorned the pitiful Colonial reproduction she was stuck with.

People are recognized as being ancient at age one hundred. The President, if he is nudged, sends birthday cards to all who reach that venerable age. Antiques, too, are officially designated as those artifacts that have been around a century or more. Perhaps it is reasonable to state that an old house at its youngest might be one hundred years old, and in its glory if it can be traced back to the eighteenth or seventeenth century. I am braced for a tirade of disagreement with this convoluted assessment of the age of an old house. It is arbitrary, at best, but a try.

The aim of this book is to outline useful techniques for solving the everyday problems of living in an old house. Many of these difficulties are indigenous to a house of any age, but all are more apt to be encountered in an old one. Remember that you are not alone. There are thousands of people just like you, many of whom are surviving in a setting older and crankier than yours. There are, however, countless feasible ways to cope with the waywardness of an old house. I hope to bring comfort to the new owner as well as the more seasoned who is baffled or insecure.

Once you have moved in and gotten over the initial

shock (and expense) of buying a new hot-water heater (they *always* need replacing, no matter how young or old), and changing most of the floats in your toilet tanks, you are ready to settle in and enjoy new surroundings. There may be other obvious needs to attend to, but they should be ignored for the time being. In fact, it is *imperative* to get used to being easygoing about repairs from the very beginning, as that is the basis for a happy life in an old house.

You know and I know some overachievers who have started pouring thousands of dollars into their old houses from the day they move in. While not flattering to the previous owner's standards, within hours it seems, the entire layout is ripped apart. Their house was, no doubt, in dreadful shape, or they may have been overanxious for the "House and Garden" effect, perhaps demanding immaculate surroundings at once. After six months when the house is perfect, they take the chance of getting bored with nothing left to do. They cannot talk to those of us who live under more marginal conditions, because we do not speak the same language. And in the end, they will never retrieve all that invested money when they sell, unless they live there forever, praying the whole time for continued inflation in the real estate market.

It is essential to do nothing (if you can) but live in your house for a year or so. Let it talk to you, penetrate you with its lore and warmth. Too-hasty repairs or changes are often regretted later. A gentleman of my acquaintance, in an effort to present his wife with one of

"central stack removed"

the finest kitchens in town, annihilated all evidence in that room that it was the oldest and most interesting part of his house. He tore out an old chimney and fireplace, complete with built-in copper kettle and beehive oven— anachronisms that had bothered him since the day he moved in. Years later, when a friend summoned the courage to tell him that he had destroyed the only fragment of worth in his entire house, he was amazed and sorry.

As you live from day to day, you will absorb enlightenment from your home, gradually pointing out the hows, wheres and whens of maintenance or renovation. No one expects you to do anything to your new (old) home for a long time. Everyone in town knows exactly how much you paid for it (they made it their business to find out), and they will naturally assume you have no money left over. Today we all pay more than we want to for any kind of housing. There is plenty of time. In fact, you will be watched like a hawk for that first visible step.

"healthy mental outlook"

1. Past Mystery

THE ORIGIN and growth of your old house was not deliberately obscured by time, only shunted into the background when too many of its inhabitants were more concerned with their narrow, apathetic daily living. Consider your ransom of the house inspired.

The pedigree of your place is much more important than the condition it is in today, whether good or bad. If it is in top form, it can go downhill fast, or if in poor repair, it can be easily fixed up. Solid construction will endure forever (barring an unforeseen catastrophe), in spite of the neglect of past owners concerned primarily with cosmetics. Actually, if all the rotten beams and timber had been replaced during its lifetime, chances are there would be nothing left to indicate age. This is the reason for new bracing and additional supports *next to* the old.

When you research your house, look for signs of

poverty. A struggling settler with the least resources was apt to put up the structure with the most integrity, because he was the one who chugged along undistracted and took his time. A wealthier man, no doubt, hurried the workmen and cut corners so he could move into his superior mansion sooner and get on with putting on the dog. After all, human nature does not change overnight, you know. And, small was beautiful back then, too. A young man started with what he could afford, rather than stretching his material thin for a larger, flimsier home. He knew that there would be time to add on since he did not expect the birth of more than one child a year.

In later houses covered with designs and ginger-bread, the chances of reliable construction were still present. A carpenter who went to the trouble of putting on yards of filigree certainly would not attach it to a building that was not meant for posterity. When you find out who put up your house, it is possible that you may also be able to determine where he came from and what he did for a living. For instance, a Puritan clergyman was probably more involved with the perpetuation and dissemination of his faith, than with his less ephemeral subsistence. On the other hand, a ne'er-do-well who had finally worked off his bondage would have stolen nothing but the best with which to construct his home.

The moment of truth came when it was time to add on and especially later, with the introduction of modern conveniences during the industrial revolution. You might find that your house incorporated the original one-room

"hollyhocks grow like crazy"

cottage into the whole, making it sturdier than the usual method of tacking on room after room. One of the sources of trouble we have now can be directly traced to the added-on kitchen. Many structural weaknesses emerged from that time. With a new fireplace to cook over, the central stack was often removed and substituted for with two chimneys, one on each side to simulate the latest style, doubling the potential for leaks and displacement of bricks.

The innovation of plumbing also underlies a good portion of our present grief. There was no way to foresee, I guess, our present handy aids such as aerosol air fresheners and the space heater, when the outhouse was moved inside. Also, we forget when we go out and spend hard-earned money on fertilizer for flower beds that the womenfolk threw dirty dishwater out the kitchen door and their hollyhocks grew like crazy. Then, too, we have had to redesign the honorable Saltbox in recent years and call it contemporary, after roofs on the original were lifted and dormers set in to expose the whole north side to penetrating winter winds.

Central heat was a good idea, but I am wondering if it was worth it for a mere hundred and fifty years. We have become so dependent and vulnerable, we may not be resilient enough to make the transition back again to the solar heating of our ancestors. Heating ducts, plumbing and wiring have weakened beams and walls that can, after all, only carry so much weight and sustain so many screw and nail holes. Man-made perforations probably far outnumber insect excavations in the wood of any given home.

Delving into the background of your house will uncover a parade of characters who passed through and left their mark. You can become acquainted with them like old relatives and weave a story linking their accomplishments together. Our house must have been hectic when in the early 1800s it was headquarters for an ambitious silkworm business that went belly up, and a hundred years later when it was home to the Ovaltine king who perfected his formula here. Every house has had its ups and downs.

What I have told you only tickles the surface of what can be learned and I wish you success as you go after that information. History creeps up on one in delightful ways through deeds, wills and local sources. Insight into the evolution of your home will help you appreciate the value of the informative architectural challenges you can look forward to. The more intimately involved you become with details of construction, reconstruction and decoration, the more you will become at one with your dwelling. Home is not where you hang your hat, it is indistinguishable from your makeup and personality and a part of every breath you take. There is no place like (an old) home!

"yes"

"no"

" quantity vs quality "

2. Buy an Old House

Upon reflection, the thought that this book might get into the hands of a reader who now lives in a new house, but has been piqued by the disquieting desire to buy an old one, has prompted me to include this information. I know that you are out there and all you may need is a little encouragement to activate this craving and fulfill a dream.

As an aside, I have been of the opinion for a long time now that a family with a number of children would be infinitely better off buying a big old house in poor condition, rather than a smaller, more pristine new one. As I dimly recall from the past, a doctor once told me that a growing family needs room, and the quality of that living space is not as important as the quantity. He felt that from a point of view of good health many large rooms with peeling wallpaper were far better than too few, well-decorated ones with everyone on top of each other. Children have a way of growing; they begin to want privacy and breathing space in which to develop their personalities. I would not push a run-down hovel on anyone, but time is on your side and a healthy family is more important than the appearance of the home in which they are brought up.

There is scant risk in buying an old house as its charm (unlike many new houses) will more than compensate for its faults. Old houses appreciate just as fast as new ones of comparable price, which makes them a sound financial investment. Ours has almost doubled in value in ten years.

The purchase of an old house (like living in one after it is yours) is not a precise science. You wear your heart on your sleeve, and well you should when taking part in an emotional experience of this magnitude. The first obstacle to overcome is location. When moving across the country or to an unfamiliar town, a decision is based upon so many factors that it is less nerve wracking to give in to the house that you fall in love with. If on the other hand you wish to remain in your home town, you have the advantage of being able to mentally stake a claim to the object of your affection and keep your eye on the newspaper, or alert a real estate agent to the house you have in mind. He can then call you when it is about to come on the market. Some owners, not scandalized, may be flattered by your interest in their home and might be talked into

"object of your affection"

giving you "first dibs," if there is a discreet way of letting them know.

Most misgivings about an old house arise when you are looking at one you have not had prior knowledge of. Inspect it on a Sunday in good weather, so you will not be distracted by the flow of commuter traffic on the street out front, or the roar of truck noise from the highway in the rear. These abrasive assaults on your sensibilities are readily overlooked after you have settled in.

Those presently in possession of your aspiration will probably be near tears at having to part with their jewel, a contingency which you have to understand and handle with subtlety. You too, could be in their shoes one day. As they reverently point out its good qualities, in their shaky state they may also acquaint you with some of its humbler characteristics, in an effort to be honest. Old-house sellers usually look buyers over as carefully as the prospective new owner is scrutinizing their home. They are suspicious, and rightly so, as they are prone to nervousness about selling to the wrong family. They want their gem in good hands and can be upset by contrary "vibes." As long as you are aware of this possibility, you can more easily adapt your own response.

When viewing a house, do not dwell on the pragmatic, or you will never be an old-house owner yourself. The majority of us are such pushovers that touring an old house is only a formality; our minds are already made up when we see the right place. Nevertheless, there is lurking in the background the feeling that we should pretend to pay attention. If you have succumbed, but think you ought to check out a few details anyway, it is quite safe to gloss over most of the bad news.

At the time we were shown one house we lived in, the owners told us about uncovering a beam in the dining room. The beam was so badly decomposed that they had decided to replace the casing and ignore it. After we bought the house and I reminded my husband of this episode, he denied any knowledge of it, a perfect example of not listening to what he did not want to hear. The beam's secret remained concealed.

Another detail that we found after moving in was the presence of fresh paint in certain rooms. It evolved in time that these were the rooms with the worst leaks. Instead of looking upon this revelation with dismay, we added the sinister idea to our own arsenal of future behavior patterns for our eventual departure. There is always light at the end of the tunnel.

On the premise that someone else's junk could be your treasure, owners should be encouraged to leave behind functional articles they no longer want, or ones that will not fit into their next house. Negotiate too, for tools and maintenance equipment they have no need for. Among other goodies, we were able to pick up at a reasonable price a lawn mower, rugs and a couple of antiques that have been indispensible.

The difference between moving into an old house or a new one is the expectation of finding trifles left behind that were not dickered for. Another positive gain is the

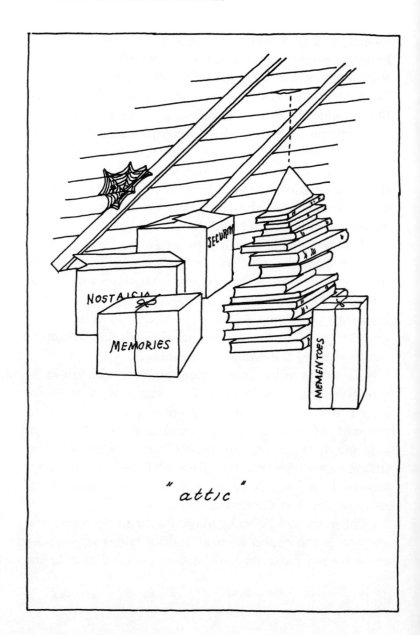

"attic"

landscaping that has been in place for so long and the pleasure and delight of watching blooms that unfold in the garden in spring. Mature foliage and old-fashioned flower beds take so many years to bear fruit, the savings in planning and planting should not be taken lightly.

There is something about an old house that makes it heartwarming and satisfying. It has an intriguing history of bustling activity, of sadness and triumph, and has spanned the lives of many good people who developed a deep affection for it when they called it home. An indefinable hint of hope permeates the air and creates a beguiling appeal that is hard to resist.

So, buy your old house—you will love it. I cannot think of a better way of putting new zest into a jaded life. You have nothing to lose and more than enough adventure ahead to spark the rest of your days.

"dropped leaf table"

3. Furnish the Rooms

FURNISHING an old house requires some manipulation plus a good dose of patience and fortitude. The main hurdle to leap and quickly put behind you is society's notion that every room has to be fully and fashionably coordinated. It is a fact that most of us move from an apartment or a small starter house to our larger old homes, and there is no possible way that the paltry number of goods we were able to gather in the past will suffice, either in amount or appropriateness, for a quainter niche.

An old house cries out for antiques and therein lies the rub. Of course you can use a combination of modern and old, or if you are not a purist, reproductions, although they are not necessarily less expensive than the real thing. One Thanksgiving when I was setting our frail, not-too-choice old dining room table, the leaf fell off. The leather chair seats were also crumbling fast. That was when we decided to get reproduction replacements, our only concession to date. The fear of a future collapse during a festive meal, upending plates and food into our guests' laps, precipitated the splurge. It is better to tread water for a while until you have a chance to recover from your move, than to rush out and spend money you do not have on furniture you may not want later.

I would start with the purchase of as many books as you can find on antique furniture, Colonial interiors, clocks, silver, period architecture and accessories. Most of these volumes are available at second-hand book stores at a decent savings over their starting price. The canvassing of used-book dealers can take many days and will, as an incidental advantage, favorably influence your friends by the thoroughness with which you are handling the assignment of appointing your home. There are any number of informative and professional authorities on these subjects and collectively the books themselves will go a long way toward the outfitting of one room, or accenting several. I am not intimating that you consider *buying* anything you see in those books, but they will certainly enhance your appreciation of what might be possible and give a clearer understanding of how to proceed.

One initial approach could be that of wearing the cloak of a Shaker for a while. By this ruse, you can manage with a minimum number of pieces for the spar-

"decorate with books"

tan look. Paint the walls and ceilings in each room white. Sand the floors, or if they do not lend themselves to this treatment, paint is more in keeping. Woodwork should be simple, either natural or painted. None of this beginning will interfere with architectural details of a specific era, for example Greek Revival or Gothic, so you can bring them into focus in succeeding more-affluent years.

Unless your neighbors get out binoculars, curtains may be forgotten (the Shakers omitted them). Otherwise, they should be muslin, plain and straight. Tall floor-to-ceiling Shaker-style cupboards and bookcases are especially useful because they can be placed to lend structural support to sagging ceilings or beams. In lieu of a resident cabinet-maker, put several unadorned chests of drawers, cabinets, or a combination on top of each other with legs cut off and apply paint. Set a pine table in the middle of the room, throw a few rag rugs around and you will have a stunning effect. A grouping of sofa and chairs before the living room fireplace, with little else, will achieve the same results. Sparsely furnished rooms have a way of becoming miraculously over-crowded with no conscious help from anyone.

The acquisition of furniture is accomplished in as many different ways as there are searchers. I was once part of a nefarious excursion in which the target was an old house in the back woods, formerly a legitimate part of the estate of one member of our group. A diminutive Cape, it was falling down with about a year of life left, but there were still some collector's items remaining inside. The senile old man who lived next door and seemed to own both places was called upon and he consented to let us in the older dwelling. He did not know when he formally unlocked the front door that we had already surveyed the terrain, gaining entrance via a gaping kitchen doorway. The first to step in fell through the floor, fortunately hitting ground a few inches below. Once inside, we rediscovered spinning wheels, books and unclaimed furniture among the debris of rags and mouse droppings. Portions of this bounty were pressed onto our doubtful claimant by the old man. I was told that at a later date another foray was made back into the house to salvage the residue. This is one way to help furnish your home, though I have mixed emotions about it. It seemed slightly less than ethical and yet all of the abandoned goods would have rotted with the place anyway, and no one would have known nor cared. I am even more dubious about poisoning your mother-in-law, however, to hasten the delivery of her collection of priceless antiques.

Let us assume that you plan to take a more normal step-by-step means of obtaining what you need. When you tire of white walls, frame some pictures and prints and move up to paisley curtains. Auctions in out-of-the-way places are still an economical way of purchasing antiques. By picking up one piece at a time you will be surprised at how fast they accumulate. The worse shape they are in and the more refinishing required, the cheaper

"Shaker - style"

they are. And, the hard work of restoration will make you feel as if you are doing your part toward the preservation of a rare and endangered species.

Another potential source of disguised antiques is the yard or garage sale, sometimes known regionally as a tag sale. I say "disguised," because a valuable desk may have had its drawer pulls replaced and be covered with many layers of paint and have wound up its latter days holding tools in a garage workshop. Early kerosene lamps are sometimes hidden under gaudy, oversized lampshades, while fine picture frames fade into the background, diminished by cheap, brightly colored country scenes of little or no intrinisic worth.

And, do not forget the dump. Many a time my opportunistic family has reported in with an unexpected windfall transferred directly from the station wagon they backed up next to. Just because a man gets as far as the dump with a load to heave out, does not mean he has made his peace with the dastardly deed. Saved at the last minute, he will leap at the chance to pass everything on unharmed to the next person in line. Others, unable to find so soft a touch on short notice, prudently leave their select collections meticulously stacked as far away as possible from the encroaching bulldozer, in the hope that their donations will be discovered and appreciated in time, or intentionally spared by a sympathetic dump keeper.

When an empty room begins to nag, buy a second-hand pool table. It will dwarf the room and promise evenings of pleasure at the same time. If there is hesitancy about the lack of aesthetic appeal, I have heard of a pool table that doubles as a dining table, making a fetching disguise as well as combining two practical pieces for the price of one. A grand piano, past its prime, will also grace a large space and motivate you to learn how to tune it and make beautiful music.

I should counsel that antiquing grows on you and can become a fever. Exploring dingy second-hand and used-furniture shops that have antiques signs out front is not only fascinating but becomes increasingly addictive. Valuable morsels are still being dug up from the bowels of these places and collectors are coy about the location of their haunts. Once having caught the disease, it is

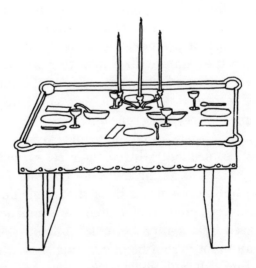

"diningroom pool table"

difficult to stop and most of the bitten keep going whether they need to or not. That is all right too, because when your house is full as I predict it will be in jig time, that is when you begin to upgrade quality. The only drawback I have found is that in replacing one item with an older, more refined specimen, one seldom disposes of the original and the house gets even more stuffed. When you reach this impasse, sell a batch of the less desirable and earn money for something more elegant. Antiquing can be a way of life and, if it does not consume you completely, is a rewarding way to spend free hours. If it does take over, well, that is the way antique shops are born.

As an old-house proprietor now, you have caught up with the rest of us, and have perhaps already felt that sinking feeling, "What hath I wrought?" Believe me, your new and unaccustomed status is not as alarming as it may seem. Help is on the way.

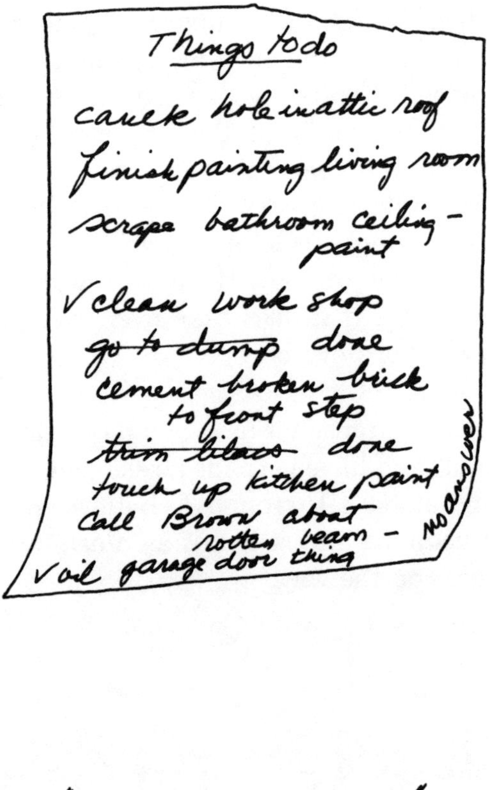

"selective neglect"

4. The Theory of Selective Neglect

T HE "golden rule" for peace of mind of old-house owners is based on the theory of selective neglect. Nearly everyone knows that there is never (a) enough time, or (b) enough money to make all necessary repairs to a house when the need first arises. And, trouble seldom occurs at well-planned intervals or judiciously chosen times. A moldering beam is almost inevitably stumbled upon on the eve of a long dreamed of (and much coveted) extended family trip. Since there is no possibility of postponing your vacation, it may be that a crisis of this nature is exactly what it takes to persuade you that your house really will not fall down in your absence. An extension of this reasoning is, of course, that it would not have caved in had you stayed at home either. The importance of accepting a reality of this enormity cannot be overestimated. It is central to the theory of selective neglect.

This theory spares you the paranoia of feeling that you have been led down the primrose path, a sensation that comes on many buyers shortly after signing final papers. It allows you to be yourself and be as irrational as you want. You may also be as inefficient as you like and eliminate errors others are snared into by panic decisions.

In order to implement the techniques of selective neglect, you must *know* what has to be done to your house and consciously say to yourself, "I will not do it." The actual needs of the house, or a sense of priorities are, therefore, mercifully and spontaneously superseded by the whim of the moment. In this way, a list of repairs may be approached randomly and any accomplishment, big or small, will bring you satisfaction and a feeling of well-being. Under this *modus operandi,* you are also perfectly free to attack symptoms and not the root cause. Inadequate problem solving is not the prerogative of any one segment of society, but is practiced with great aplomb by many businesses and institutions, with government at all levels particularly adept at it. This attitude had been a tradition in my home long before we arrived on the scene.

A healthy mental outlook about yourself and your home is inevitable if you religiously adhere to the tenets of the theory of selective neglect. This is not saying that there will not be ample to keep you busy in your spare time, so no one can accuse you of being lazy or, conversely, of showing off by overdoing in haste or hysteria.

" slightly seedy look "

There are several good reasons for adopting this way of life, aside from the most important one of being less harried. It automatically averts any chance of attracting attention. Neighbors and friends, even relatives, can get very uneasy if they see you making the slightest improvement to your home. You can also bring on a feeling of hopeless inadequacy in people you do not even know. If you find that you have to tackle a major problem area, try to confine it to the back of the house, or if it must be seen, be as subtle as possible. You might do the job on a long weekend when everyone is away.

Another reason for remaining inconspicuous is the possibility of burglary. It is far better to maintain a slightly seedy look to your place, than take the chance of losing anything of sentimental value inside. Thieves are likely to look for signs of prosperity and will almost certainly pass you by if you have been careful to avoid the "moneyed" look. Then there is the tax assessor to outfox. His eyes are sharp and if he thinks for a minute that you have done something, anything, to your house, he will pay you a visit.

Tranquility will be your reward for being yourself and not worrying excessively about what others think or say. Remember that you *could* have bought a perfectly dull and unimaginative brand-new dwelling, but instead you opted (and so did I) to buy an old one with character and nooks and crannies. Enjoy the eccentricities of your home. Do not let it nag you. If you allow one problem to get under your skin, others will be sure to follow and you will become unhinged all too soon. It is remarkably comforting to realize how much tougher and more resourceful we are than our ancestors, in spite of their superior reputation. After all, our houses were new when they lived in them and we all know it is much easier to live in a new house than an old one.

"tax assessor"

"warm summer day"

5. Time Management

W‌HILE I realize it is difficult for some people to relax in a house that needs work, try not to let goal-setting hinder any normal tendency toward procrastination, nature's way of doubting the worth of those goals in the first place. House restoration should never take precedence over nap-taking, for instance, since rejuvenation of body and soul is just as vital, if not more so. When a warm summer day stretches out in front of you and you feel overcome with inertia, resting in the sun to fall asleep over a good book is salutory. Winter is irrevocably coming and with it the end of this sort of choice.

Resist, too, letting the needs of your house cause you complete paralysis. It is wisest in this case to go away for the weekend. Take the time to get a change and learn to rearrange priorities until you can face your house with equanimity. Upon your return, everything will be as it was when you left, only the curse should be lifted, leaving the jobs to be done wearing a sweeter scent.

Overhaul your "gotta list," that slip of paper on which you have written things to do. My husband is a master at manipulating his list. Those tasks that are clearly the most distasteful or time consuming get relegated to the bottom of the pile and he finds that with frequent rewriting, they are easily moved off completely. Thus, the remaining assignments become markedly more palatable. A few minutes spent refining a list can save hours of labor and lighten your perspective as well.

Time management is a must for housewives also. The number of ways you can save time or use it to better advantage are endless. First of all you have to be tough, almost heartless, in giving up some of the old-fashioned routines your mother and grandmother performed. I have always considered it a criminal waste of time to make the beds every day. After all, they will be ripped open and slept in again in a few short hours, only to be put back together the next morning.

You do not have to wash the dishes after every meal. Breakfast and lunch dishes are so minor that it does them no harm to soak in the sink until dinner preparation time. Then, there is the hopeless ritual of ironing. I can remember seeing sheets, hankies and even underwear go under the iron. Sometimes I forget and buy something that is not drip dry and cause no end of trouble for myself. If you run out of this and that, make do with substitutes.

Peripheral "ought tos" (I ought to wash the curtains) that are left undone, probably did not need doing anyway and the proof is that life goes on whether or no. The shock-of-neglect factor is in your own head. Just ask yourself if anyone noticed or complained; my guess is that no one was the wiser.

The delegation of authority and use of subordinates are also important time management concepts of value. Put your children to work by coercion or bribery. It is never too late to instill the work ethic in the young, a principle they will thank you for later when they are old enough to forgive past injustices.

These, and perhaps other ideas that you have tucked away in the back of your mind but did not dare pay heed to are all smart ways of restructuring your life to avoid being so neurotic that you cease to enjoy your old house. If the fundamentals of time management hinge on "doing the most important things first," then it is up to all of us to be frank with ourselves and not be trapped by tradition or what the neighbors might say.

Old houses are used to being patient, because they know that they did not reach the level of esteem they experience today by being fussed over at the drop of a hat. They do not hold grudges, are proud and content simply to be loved during those intervals of inaction.

"wild screaming fight"

6. Who Does the Work?

ULTIMATELY the day will come, despite your best intentions, when you will have to perform some surgery on your house. The question then becomes not one of shall we or shan't we but who will do the work. Rate busters are not appreciated in the world of home repairs. While we may pretend to be envious of the home owner who has endless talents and is skilled in all phases of carpentry, brick work and plumbing, our repressed feelings of hostility may surface to mar an otherwise fruitful relationship with that individual. So, please, play down any superiority in this field.

On the average, any one of us is capable of some repair work, although time is worth money and many find it more politic to hire to have the work done, than do it themselves. A simple phone call to your local contractor, however, may not do the trick. In the first place, most reputable contractors have more business than they can handle fixing up everyone else's old houses. A secretary may be optimistic about the chances of her boss calling you back, but the odds are not in your favor. It may take repeated calls to get any attention.

Then again, there are certain jobs like operating on a leaky roof that a few companies not only instinctively shy away from if they find out the house is old, but may even give you a flat no, without so much as offering to look at the ailing area. It is sad, but true, that not everyone will consider it a privilege to work on your beautiful home, and even an offer of free cocktails and dinner at the end of each shift would not change their minds. They are looking for easy hassle-free jobs anyway, and are not the adventurous type of people you need. Cheer up, though, there is someone out there daring enough to help you— willing to be diverted from the humdrum of an ordinary work day. Persevere.

If, by some haphazard quirk, you do gain the attention of a contractor who agrees to help you out, ascertain whether or not he knows the building inspector. Building inspectors can wield unheard-of power and are apt to be intimidating. I once went through a very ticklish two hours when a contractor invited one in to study my house. It was like having the Vicar to tea and being questioned on my failure to show at church every Sunday. I was put in a position where a critical examination of my house and its faults became an oblique scrutiny of me, and I was hard pressed to be pleasant and appreciative. The building inspector told me that he had the authority to condemn a house and throw out the owners, if conditions were too dangerous or unsanitary. Mindful of my own culpability, I was, admittedly, cowed.

There are other ways, too, of hiring help. You might seriously consider going the young-couple route. These days, quite a number of college graduates or late dropouts who (disbelieving their parents' view that the sure way to heaven is through advanced degrees) have become highly adept at the building trades. These young people are intelligent and tolerant and, above all, intrepid. We once enjoyed the company of a very special pair who agreed on one occasion to babysit as they worked on the house, while my husband and I skipped out for a week of vacation.

Along with our couple came other surprises worth the inconvenience of two more mouths to feed, if you find that a deterrent. We had the honor of meeting their enormous Great Dane. Our two cats were terrified at finding such a large creature in *their* bailiwick. In an effort to rout him out by hissing and growling, they succeeded only in scaring each other into a wild, screaming fight under his feet. Although slightly unnerved by the noise, he never saw the cause of it, he ranged so high above the floor.

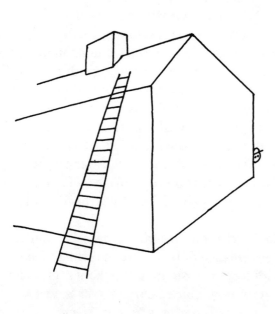

"acrophobia"

7. The Exterior of Your House

THERE IS HARDLY a house from the past that is today the same form or size as the day it was built, and those with added ells or wings, fractured roofs and "new" dormer windows are harder to keep track of than when they were simple. The outside of all these places has weathered the onslaught of rain, snow, sleet, and hail on "bad days" and on the good, has absorbed rays of the sun to dry up under fair skies. The southern façade has suffered a complete change from wet to hot sun, over and over, while the north has faced stronger winter storms and has seen little or no sun. Our old houses have repeatedly been harassed and we have the legacy of this turmoil: peeling paint in front, decay in the rear and a serenely disintegrating roof on top.

Roof

The roof of your house can be one of its most fascinating and unpredictable features. The multi-level variety, a result of roof-raisings and add-ons, are often objects of great beauty in contrast to their more elementary single-pitch cousins. They can also be more puzzling. Foreknowledge of the pitfalls of assaulting any roof configuration will allow you to approach it with sensitivity and caution.

At the very least, your roof may spit shingles, or at its worst, develop a massive hemorrhage. The odd gap up there can be safely overlooked for years, depending on your schedule or feelings of acrophobia. When the time comes that you are ready to fill in the holes, it is probable that the old shingles, even if you can find them on the ground, will be impaired beyond use. A sensible and less-ostentatious alternative to the insertion of unweathered new ones, is the shifting of old ones from a back roof somewhere out of sight. Those spaces, in turn, can be filled in at your leisure.

A roof with one or more leaks presents a greater challenge. Think twice, however, before being tempted to scrap the whole roof for a new one. Such a precipitous action may be completely unnecessary and the attendant expense could cripple your bank account for years, as well as reduce your ability to take advantage of more interesting ways of spending that money in the future.

The use of pails, kettles and baby bathtubs is an age-old and well-respected method of catching water inside your home. I mention baby bathtubs because their extra length can sometimes span several isolated drips. We found a forgotten one in our California cellar that we knew would come in handy some day. It is made of enamelware and attractively ornamented with scenes from Mother Goose nursery rhymes. A padding of terry toweling in each receptacle will mute the sound and limit the height of the splash. If the leak is not severe, the water in the pail will probably evaporate between storms to evenly humidify your rooms, and be of very little concern indefinitely. You may have to take heavier leaks more seriously, especially if they occur in your dining room, for instance, and it happens to downpour on the evening of a dinner party that there is no way of deferring at the last minute. (Keep in mind, however, that a trumped-up excuse for postponement can be done smoothly and without suspicion, in a pinch. Mention a dead mouse in the heating duct and an unpleasant effluvium.)

As long as the leakage does not inordinately disturb your daily life, it is advisable to let it continue in order to have a maximum amount of time to study the problem. Identification of the source of any leak can take years in some cases, but it is not difficult to adjust your life to a temporary rearrangement of furniture to accommodate pails and buckets when called for. There is definite prestige (if you have lived in your house for some time), in pointing out a leak to your friends and explaining that the origin has yet to be found. This is one way of warding off a prejudgment on the ratty condition of your wall-paper.

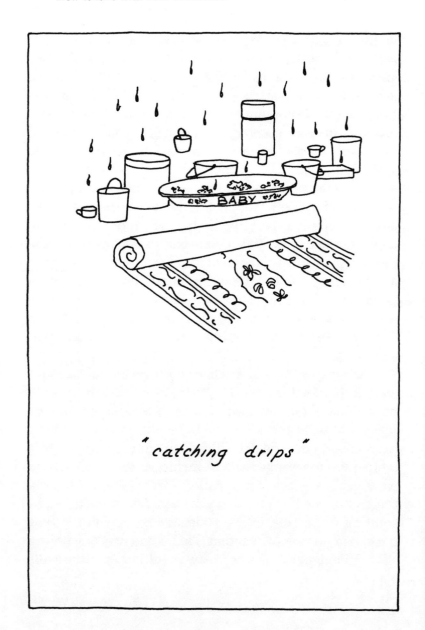

"catching drips"

Rumor has it that a certain government building, erected in Boston in the late '60s, has a very stubborn roof leak. Not only was the cause never established, the search has been discontinued in favor of pizza pan sled collectors re-directing the flow of water through attached hoses to a newly installed permanent drain.

When you are sufficiently stimulated to act, keep your remedies modest. Usually it is better to patch first before moving on to more elaborate schemes. By patching, you will be able to circumvent the annoyance of applying for a building permit at the town hall. Some towns require this document in order to "keep track of the number of layers of material on all roofs." (There is some question in my mind as to how effective this method of control is. No one I know has ever applied for one except

"a respectable slope"

me, and I was denied it the first time because I could not come up with the total of square feet involved.)

Patching usually means the use of more of the same substance that is already up there. If it is a flat roof with tar and stones, more of that is applied, or if shingles, these are neatly laid over the section under suspicion. The joining area of roofs with different levels should be minutely examined, as leaks can often be ascribed to careless work there, inadequate flashing or shoddy workmanship.

In the event that your house leaks as badly after patching as it did before, you have the choice of re-covering the entire roof or taking everything off and starting fresh. I have been in the enviable position of experiencing both of the above alternatives.

Stripping a roof is exciting because it opens up a chance to see the original construction and you can appreciate its sturdiness in comparison to contemporary work. Also, you have an opportunity to understand the fascination that some town fathers have with the various strata. In our case, there were seven in all, and what had appeared to be a nearly flat roof boasted a very respectable slope when finally exposed. The many applications of tar and stones gave way to two coverings of ancient wood shingles before the base of horizontal boards (pitted with nail holes) was reached. We felt much safer with this unnecessary weight removed.

The final step of re-roofing is quite straightforward, as is the laying of an entire roof with its second coat of shingles. About the only variable is the flashing. On the front of a house where it can be seen, you may be seduced by copper which definitely has more class than its less expensive alternate, aluminum. Do not use it to excess (it may be too showy) and make sure that the green it will eventually turn to, harmonizes with the color scheme of your exterior.

There is one crucial aspect of all this re-roofing activity you should be particularly careful to keep in sight. *Do not* allow yourself to be lulled into a sense of security about your new house top, or sections thereof. If you are lucky, your leaks may be gone, or at least significantly abated. On the other hand, you could find, as we did, that your new topping appears to do little more than filter the moisture to a finer degree. While we were grateful for purer drips and somewhat less volume, we realized that our ingenuity was to be truly tested and that we still had plenty of time to readjust our thinking to come up with a more suitable answer.

Chimneys

A house without at least one chimney looks naked. Truthfully, the most popular feature we all look for, in buying an old house, are the fireplaces. Unfortunately, a poorly maintained chimney is a real fire hazard. On the other hand, if you do not use your fireplaces, you will not have to worry so much about the condition of the chimneys. A fireplace is pleasing, even when not in use. Adorn

"enchanting fireplaces"

it with a fan or a casual pile of birch logs and visitors cannot help but be enchanted. It is *de rigueur* today to conserve precious heat in winter by sealing up all fireplaces, either with built-in dampers or a piece of plywood across the face to double as a display board for Christmas cards.

In case you cannot resist lighting a fire once in a while, you should probably take a glance down your chimney. As in everything else, there are those who know how to clean and fix their own chimneys. My inclination is to forgive them if they have a knack for it. The rest of us have to run our fingers through the yellow pages and hope for the best. However, pointing (the technical term for scraping out cracked mortar from between bricks and replacing it with new) is a finicky and sometimes dangerous craft, costly enough to make it worth your while to call friends for a referral.

If you are able to get to your chimney before too many bricks have fallen off, you will be spared the chagrin of being arrested (as a friend of mine nearly was) trying to pick up a load of the used variety from someone's country cellar hole or private dump. Regrettably, some chimneys are so decrepit they have to be completely rebuilt from the roof up. There is nothing that looks worse than a new chimney on an old house, especially if you have been careful to preserve a low profile. That is about the only incentive to face chimney work at an early stage of disrepair.

Chimneys that are used with any amount of frequency must be cleaned every few years. And cleaning is

"chimney sweep"

expensive. Still, chimney sweeps, notably the young ones, have upgraded their image and become so jaunty with Dickensian top hats and tails that they must be a joy to have around. We had our young couple point and clean our chimneys as well as have "a go" at the roof, so we were deprived of colorful clothing. They toyed with the idea of straightening one chimney, although its rakish angle was a hallmark of the house. Incredibly, they found the chimney much more sound than it looked from the ground and decided against it. We probably could have held off on the rest of the work for a while longer.

One other problem that some people have with chimneys is a gap that can develop around the base at roof level, if the house is susceptible to the buffeting of strong winds. There is a goo that can be applied which has the lovely attribute of remaining semi-viscous in consistency while at the same time adhering to chimney and roof or flashing. I have heard that this preparation really works.

Siding

A good coat of paint on the outside of your house will cover a multitude of sins. But, for heaven's sake, do not put it on all at once unless you have to. The cost can be as debilitating as that of a complete roof job. There are other pitfalls.

My neighbors, charmed by a group of "nice" painters, were hoodwinked into letting them paint the whole outside of their pretty litte Cape with latex paint, unaware that it would not bond with the oil that was underneath. The painters were safely out of town by the time the discovery was made and my neighbors were faced with a costly repainting job in a very short time.

By covering one or two sections annually, you can, in a manner of speaking, amortize the cost over a time span of several years. (You could employ the less-expensive substitute—ivy. Ivy grows fast and will produce dense cover in a short time. Colleges and private schools are fond of the ivy cover-up solution.)

Scraping and painting a house is tedious and boring, but some roving bands of high school boys are good at it and eager for the money. Let them turn up their radios and they will work like beavers. A word of caution: discourage their scraping too vigorously or they might

"let them turn up their radios"

uncover an acute situation you would rather they had not. One of the last group of boys to help us was a member of his high school gymnastics team and had pumped his share of iron. His scraper skidded off the edge of a clapboard and straight into the house. A large area of dry rot had osmosed from an internal post through the clapboards (or from clapboard to post) the size of which we are reluctant to pin down. Luckily this distressing blight was discovered behind a blind (or shutter) which was quickly swung back into place, in the hope that with nature's amnesia we would be able to overlook it. (If the theory of selective neglect has ever worked for us, it is working now, except that it has not been easy to forget such an unattractive malignancy.) Dry rot is insidious, because while the wood in the affected zone looks almost healthy, it is a sham and there is little else to do but replace it.

In a brighter vein, however, have faith that the only patches of misery will be a defective clapboard, here and there, that can easily be swapped for pre-painted new ones, and work can progress on schedule. (Pre-painting helps to prevent warping.) After scraping, if necessary, get your boys to do some caulking. Specialists on the subject sometimes recommend that toothpicks be placed under each clapboard at regular intervals to help the circulation of air and foil the numerous kinds of decay that threaten our existence. This may work if everything is wholesome underneath. We found, to our enormous gratitude (sure that all was not satisfactory be-

"only a couple of months"

neath), that caulking the cracks of the overlapping clapboards in the vicinity of our presumably porous roof proved to be the perfect answer to our major leaks. What luck! Evidently the ice dams (beefy mountains of snow and ice at the edge of a roof) had curled over the rim and down the side of the house, and in melting had backed up through the cracks between the clapboards and into the house.

Some houses lend themselves to being shingled. These, too, can be redone one or two sides at a time, if need be, only I wish you would not paint the shingles because that defeats the purpose of using wood with its natural water shedding qualities.

On the subject of aluminum or vinyl siding: forget it. It is much too easy and nothing important can go wrong with it. Besides, it is expensive to install and not authentic for an old house.

Blinds

Of all the inventions of mankind, blinds rank among the highest in nuisance value. (Some people call them shutters. Some call them worse names.) First of all, they shake loose and blow in the wind at night—always in the middle of the night, never during the day, no matter how windy it is. Secondly, with no provocation whatsoever, they fall off. And thirdly, either on the house or off, the little slats loosen and sag to eventually slip out and evaporate.

Woe betide the homeowner who neglects to retrieve a fallen blind. Although ours had been leaning against the house only a couple of months, the mischief done was incredible and will require hours of labor to repair. If you are ever in such a predicament, the simplest way to resolve it is to take down all the other blinds on your house. Their usefulness for closing on hot days to shade a room, which is I suppose what they were intended for, has long ago been obfuscated by combination storm windows that use up the assigned space. You will never miss them and will soon adjust to the cleaner, neater lines. I wish we could have done this, but we were handicapped by the need to conceal the post and clapboards, disfigured by dry rot.

Ivy and wisteria have a propensity for entwining tendrils through blind louvers and splitting them apart, with the wisteria growing oversized, making it impossible to pull out. Several of my blinds bulge with gnarled pieces of vine even though the stalk no longer climbs near.

Blinds were not in common use prior to 1800, but they have a way of complimenting some houses and endearing themselves to us. And, like the builders permit in some towns, permission for their removal must be sought in parts of others from an Historic Districts Commission, arbiters of local taste.

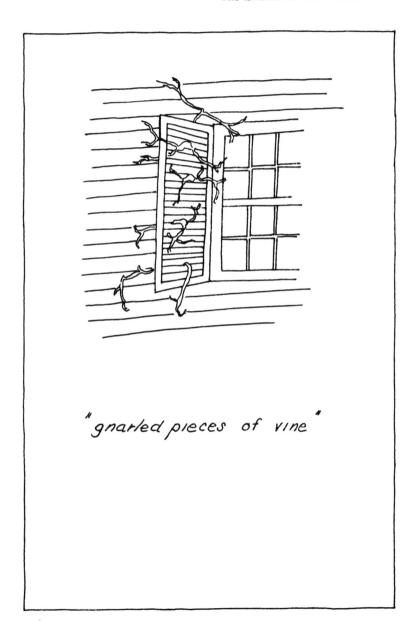

"gnarled pieces of vine"

Porches

Porches are provocative because they require a never-ending imagination to keep intact. They were almost always tacked on as an afterthought when someone tired of not having that small fragment of shelter while going out of the house on a stormy day.

As an appendage, a porch is overexposed to the ravages of wind, rain, snow and honey bees that enjoy boring holes for their hives in hollow columns. Brick or stone steps are a prerequisite, as steps are the first element of a porch to go. Not long after they have disappeared, you may have an opportunity to become acquainted with the manner in which the roof was attached to the house. If you had an imperfect knowledge of flashing before you bought your old house, you will become an expert on all phases of its use very quickly. When the paint on the ceiling starts peeling and the boards warp, you can generally assume that the flashing is no longer doing its duty. Or, it may be the porch underpinning sagging, forcing the roof to part from the house.

The thought of putting time and money into a dinky porch may stretch your good humor somewhat, but it has been my observation that porches are worth saving and I strongly recommend their resuscitation. They are a convenient place to store the milk box and snow shovels in winter. My cats appreciate ours most on a rainy day, because they can be outdoors, hunched up and miserable, instead of inside, while they wait for the sun to come out.

"rainy day"

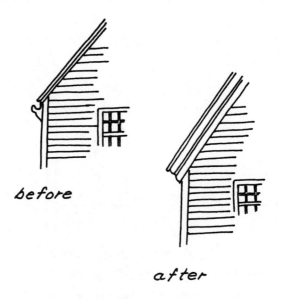

before

after

"lower your blood pressure"

When a larger porch decides to slump, it may not merit the expense of reconstruction. This decision would depend, perhaps, on whether you can effect a truce with your mosquito population. We have a convenient raised section of patio which was once encircled by a porch. The mosquitoes win as dusk begins to fall.

Gutters

Under certain circumstances, gutters may be worth putting up with, although little apparent research has been done to improve their behavior. At some period in the life of our house, someone lowered his blood pressure significantly by extending the roof down over all of the wooden gutters, sealing them off forever. This left only one metal fossil in the rear to worry about, which aimed the runoff directly into the cellar.

It may be that you have a long-standing reverence for gutters which inhibits your ability to eliminate them entirely. Or, possibly the overhang of your roof is not bold enough to prevent the water from running down the outside. Your only alternative then, is to keep them in place and follow the autumn ritual on tipsy ladder to remove each year's accumulation of leaves or pine needles. I have seen a house that had an overflow of several year's collection and a magnificent growth of tall weeds marching up the roof. Moss, for the devotee, will also grow luxuriously in a gutter.

In all but the mildest climates, there is another seasonal threat more difficult to deal with and that is the ubiquitous ice dam. If you have extra cash and have figured out the secret code that will bring a roof man to your home, zigzag wires across the border, dipping into the gutter and out the downspout, evidently help. See that he runs the wire through a junction box with a light as well as a switch, to remind you not to leave the system

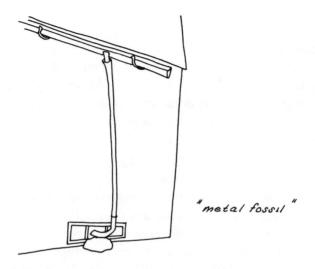

" metal fossil "

on all summer. Short of this modern miracle, you will
have to join the rest of us with shovel and broom in the
sunny aftermath of each winter storm to knock off the
snow along the edges.

Garage

A garage may have been designed to house the
family car or cars, but its real purpose is for storage in
anticipation of a garage sale. Any garage worth its salt is
full of old furniture, lawn tractors, mini-bikes, snow-
blowers, bicycles, rakes, shovels, tools and one or more
canoes. The reason for this is that it is safer to have a car
in the driveway to pretend that someone is always at
home.

66

You may, if you have two cars, want to try to keep one in the garage. I have been moderately successful, although the effort has caused me to be more of a shrew than I normally like to be. It is difficult to know if the end justifies the means. I am certain, however, that if you allow the smallest wedge between your car and its rightful space, the entire area will fill instantly, with no feelings of remorse on anyone's part.

Though a garage may seem peripheral to life in your old homestead, its problems have a way of intruding daily, and should not be slighted. Our woodpile has yet to make it into the garage, an objective held in abeyance.

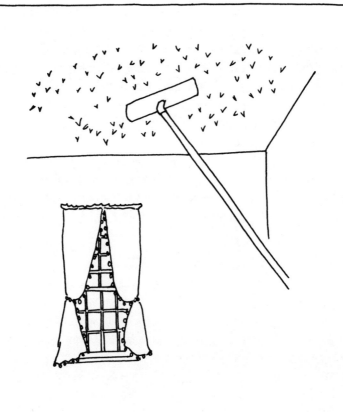

"vacuum your ceiling"

8. The Interior of Your House

WHILE THE OUTSIDE of your house has been subjected to the stress of atmospheric vagaries, sun and frost for all these years, the inside has absorbed the shocks of its inhabitants. The young have been running up and down stairs, playing hide and seek in the dark, bouncing on beds, missing in the bathrooms and scoring everywhere else with illicit games of ball and other boisterous high jinks. And adults were walking around in heavy boots, steaming in showers, smoking and moving furniture about to add and subtract from rooms. Pets too, of every kind, have used their claws without discretion. It is no wonder we are busy today, trying to keep our homes livable.

Ceilings

Ceilings should be easy. They are not holding anything up and they are out of the way. But, I have never lived in a house where the ceilings were able to control themselves. They peel, sag, drip water, crack and fall down. This has nothing to do with the fact that I am not a conscientious housekeeper—it is simply the nature of ceilings.

Some ceilings peel for obscure reasons. My daughter's bedroom is located under a tight, dry attic and yet she complains of waking in the morning with her hair full of paint chips. My bedroom ceiling, next door under the same uncorrupt attic, has peeled very little, even where it has been battered by small children jumping up to test their height. The finger prints remain and so does the paint.

Other ceilings erupt for a good and obvious cause. Fortunately, overflowing bath tubs, sinks and toilets can be quickly identified and adjustments made. Vaporizers are extremely hazardous and for the same steamy reason, bathroom ceilings tend to mildew as well as peel. I try to wait for the mildew to come off with the paint, so I will be able to go on from there.

You may want to help the peeling process by vacuuming your ceiling from time to time. If you have the patience, as my mother did, eventually the whole ceiling will clean itself. It took her many years of regular vacuuming, but in the end her reward was a surface ready for new paint without the bother of scraping and sanding.

The worst cases of peeling, cracking or sagging are, of course, caused by our old avenger, the leaky roof. My son's bedroom ceiling (under a less reliable roof than his

"against future buildup"

sister's) developed an alarming bulge and finally began to dump quantities of rain water on to the bottom of his bed. When he got cold feet and moved out, the decision to remove the entire ceiling quickly followed. The room is small so the task was not difficult: I stuffed my husband and our three children in, shut the door and they worked off years of aggression bashing down that ceiling. Afterward, we marked drips with chalk in a futile effort to define the direction and scope of the leak. It was at this point that we decided to do something to the roof. We now have a restored ceiling, thanks to our young couple.

If you can get to the ceiling earlier, I have another suggestion. In our kitchen, there was an offensive, circular discoloration which I had almost succeeded in camouflaging with many applications of paint. Then one horrible night, water crept along the upside (causing a shallow dip) and through a hole where there had once been a light fixture. It overflowed an antique glue pot hung directly underneath that was filled with cooking utensils. The next morning, with daring and great skill, my husband swiftly drilled a hole at the apex of the sag with a three-quarter-inch bit. We thought there was still water in there but none came out, which was somewhat of a disappointment. We are taking no chances, however, and have installed a cork in the hole against future buildup.

I can now report that the cork is doing a fine job also of trapping moist air above the ceiling which in turn has caused the paint to peel over the entire surface. We are currently holding a national contest to see who can submit the largest single flake and encourage anyone who wants to enter to send in their sample to be measured against ours. I would advise you that competition is very rough and the winner will not be announced until after we move out of the house.

My examples are extreme so you can see that a mere crack in your ceiling is nothing to worry about. Ceiling cracks are usually caused by a definite bias stress on your house and for whatever reason, (perhaps nothing more than a howling north wind) if filled and painted, will re-open in the same place time and again. So, save your anxiety and energy for other proofs of patience.

As to painting ceilings, watch the kind of paint you use. Even as the outside of your home will peel if you apply latex over oil-base paint (or oil over latex), inside surfaces are just as vulnerable. I have had success in some rooms with latex, but in others which must have been last done with oil the latex refused to stick and I was soon back where I began.

Walls and Windows

Wallpaper will cover irregularities in your walls. Paint is easier to apply and keep clean. The people who lived in and loved my home adored wallpaper and plenty of it. I stripped eight layers from my dining room walls, with some duplications, as though the paper was so precious they could not bear to cover it with another pattern. One might have thought that in such quantity the wallpaper was holding up the walls, although that was not true, except in isolated spots where some of the plaster was liberated with the paper.

When you remove wallpaper and find the plaster pockmarked with holes, large or small, use this condition as an excuse to brush up on your patching technique. Large holes can be squared off and fitted with a piece of plaster board, pre-cut. Then mix spackling powder to a gooey consistency and lather it over the area with a broad plasterer's trowel. Some of the picture-hanging cavities can be dabbed with a putty knife. Be sure to leave a few dents or the wall will begin to look new. When all is dry, a little sandpaper and a lot of sneezing will ready it for paint. This operation is not half as fussy as it may sound, because spackling compound is compassionate and will not allow you to make a tragic mistake.

Noises in walls that sound like mice keeping house probably are just that. Some cats will eliminate the problem for you, though I have found my pair useless in that regard. It is not a mouse to them, unless it comes from outdoors and can be properly offered up to me on the kitchen doormat, for effusive praise.

Windows that are not opened in the summer do not require their storm windows removed. When it became less fashionable to live in dark houses, someone took out our antiquated, undersized windows and put in the largest, most ill-proportioned ones that money could buy. As a result, the combination storm windows are so heavy I can hardly lift them. Strictly speaking, half of our storms are a sort of semi-combination in that with windows six over nine, eight over twelve or twelve over sixteen, the bottom storm window has to be removed in order to slide the screen into the same space. Those windows are ungainly and unbelievably heavy. *I* have to install and remove them, because it takes an extraordinary amount of patience, more than anyone I know can muster. To save on my own wear and tear, I have developed the viable system of changing only the ones we actually open in summer, considerably less than half the grand total on the house.

Floors and Doors

In contrast to popular belief, not every old house has lovely wide pine floor boards. If I go into my cellar and look up, I can see my massive beauties. It is a shame that they are at the bottom of the heap. What I have to work with are narrow, unsightly and not all going in one direction as so many changes have been made to the interior of our home. There are thin strips of wood in the cracks where the boards have shrunk away from each other, and since they are loose, they squeak gleefully as they shoot up clouds of dust when walked on. The only recourse with floors of this ilk is to paint them.

And then there are the "Lally columns" that support so many old houses. The theory behind their use must surely be to level sagging floor beams. In our house, for

"past errors in judgement"

some unknown reason, they are cranked up so high that we have mountains and valleys to walk on. The experience is exhilarating.

There are times in the life of a house when some doors will not open and others will not close. Wait a few months and the situation may be reversed. This phenomenon can sometimes be attributed to over-ambitious seasonal winds that tilt a house one way part of the year and the other way the rest. My mother, whose house is more stable than it sounds (I hope), plans on foregoing the use of her front door six months of each year because the prevailing northerly winter winds tip her house just enough to put it out of commission. She knows by now that the lack of a functioning front door is a minor inconvenience compared with sticky bedroom doors when the tables are turned and southwest winds take over in summer.

In a house with a seemingly permanent cant, it is tempting to shave door tops and edges in order to coerce them into their alloted slots. The wisdom of this move is dubious, however, since the warp may be self-correcting, in time. We have several doors that have been transformed from rectangles to rhomboids, although the doorways are true. We also have doors with strips of wood tacked on to the top and bottom to make up for past errors in judgment.

Lally columns again may be at fault. An uplift caused by over-bracing may distort door frames and cause no end of grief. Check the height of your cellar before augmenting or sawing off doors. You might consider dispensing with some doors altogether. Most houses have too many, anyway. We found an eclectic assortment in our cellar when we moved in, evidence of the insight of former owners.

The newer your old house, the higher the ceilings and doorways are apt to be, but older houses with multi-layered floors have a predisposition to doorways that "zap" you in the forehead. Since I am short, I sail right through any doorway. My boys, alas, have to stoop as they enter their bedrooms and very soon I expect them to develop premature bald spots from grazing their heads on the ceilings. Our cellar stairs, also, are not designed for sprightly descent and I cringe as I anticipate cries of pain when metermen brave the depths to collect their data.

Plumbing

When I see my husband walk through the room with a determined look on his face and dozens of wrenches under his arm, I know it is time to leave and visit a friend, and the sooner the better. Recalcitrant plumbing is the bane of his life.

Every old house has its quota of tired pipes and fixtures, and although any housewife can learn to change a faucet washer, the worst is always yet to come. I will never forget the feeling of sheer fright when I discovered a sewer pipe in the cellar of one house we lived in that

" snake "

had already been wrapped with patching in several places and was clearly in the throes of death. I am not sure which scared me more, the thought of raw sewage gushing all over the basement, or the cost of replacing that pipe.

Even the relatively easy task of cleaning out a sink trap is a nightmare. The snake, contrary to instructions, will not turn corners; its tail succeeds only in strangling the throw rug as it slaps the ceiling. For some reason, we are sold snakes that are way too long and should be cut in half before use. When you give up on the snake and open the trap, it seems as though the pail to catch the flow will never be large enough, and there is seldom any sealing compound in the house to secure the joint again. Make certain your equipment is adequate before starting.

Practicing what I preach, I once replaced the washers

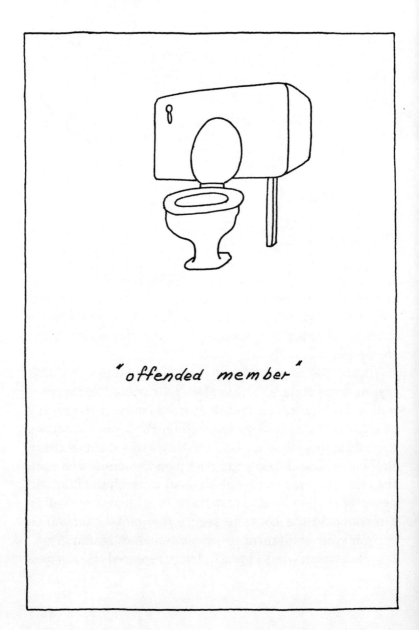

"offended member"

in the kitchen sink taps. The new ones failed to stem the trickle from the independent spout set between the two. Egged on by my husband, I moved on to the more abstruse task of dismantling the spout itself and was rewarded with complete satisfaction. There were several pieces left over when I had it reassembled, but I concluded they were extras, because the faucet has not dripped since. A fine spray squirts up from the housing to atomize my hanging plant now and then, so on the whole I have no complaints.

It is the vintage toilets that send my husband into a tizzy. He cannot bear it when they malfunction even though he has become quite skilled at titivating hardware inside the tanks. In a recent battle with his nemesis, he almost lost. Having successfully replaced a double-threaded section of pipe leading from the "flush tank" (no mean feat), he managed to lean too heavily on that tank and dislodge it from the wall. I am sure he said what he thought was his final prayer and mentally double checked last will and testament. When I arrived on the scene, though, all was quiet; a two-by-two was neatly supporting the offended member and my hubby was in the kitchen, dosing himself generously with Librium. Able at last to look back in amusement at that day, he is now trying to decide what color he should stain the prop.

The best defense against any unruly bathroom is to close the door and keep an "out of order' sign on it for the duration. If you have only one bathroom, build a new one immediately. I do not know what to suggest when an upstairs shower springs a leak, except that perhaps that is when you take in your shingle and prepare to sell and move to another house.

Heat

Unless you want an excuse to take to your bed permanently say no to the man who snaps infrared pictures of the outside of old houses. He is the killjoy who exposes heat loss. You have enough cares without being snidely apprised of the extent to which you are helping to heat all out-of-doors. Though he may mean well, he is no more than a pettifogging troublemaker.

When you find time, read the newspapers and look for some woodland to buy. The money expended can be thought of as an investment in two ways: for firewood now and evermore, plus future building lots for your children. A five-acre parcel has been said to yield a lifetime of wood for one family, provided it is properly harvested. Insurance like this guarantees flexibility, both for supplementing your heat today and as a fallback position when we run out of fossil fuels.

Having made alternative plans, you can go ahead and add more insulation to the mouse-ravaged corn cobs in the walls of the house. (Corn cobs and rubble brick were favored early on.) I would assume that some past owner has already thought of doing this and you should only have to consolidate his contribution to fit in more of your own. The mice may be briefly disoriented, but rest assured, they will make a total recovery. You need the additional heat of their warm bodies as well as a circulation of air through their tunnels.

If you run short of cash, close off all the north-side rooms and concentrate your living where the sun shines in giving hope and enrichment. Should the move involve your kitchen, cooking over a fireplace will furnish valuable insight into the constitution of our foremothers. Later perhaps, you can finish insulating, or open up the whole south side with floor-to-ceiling double-glazed windows for passive solar heat, and forget the rest.

Since the subject is brought up, we better get on with storm windows, the vexation of which I have already alluded to. They are necessary, as a friend of mine who acquiesced found out, after years of objecting that they

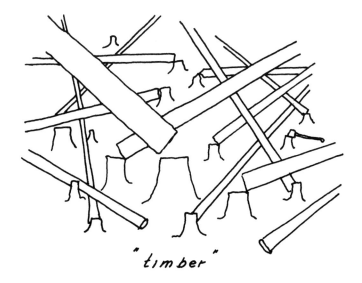

"timber"

defaced the distinguished lines of her classical home. Although they discourage some of the cold air from coming in, I have noted that the "weep holes," even if I can find them, are never free from obstruction and the build-up of melt water toward the sill leaks down through my walls to the destruction of heaven knows what. An awl is your tool here. We put storm windows on our bedrooms and then crack them for fresh air at night, so I am not clear as to what this means to their over-all efficiency.

Fireplaces for those unfortunate individuals who did not plan ahead and purchase a private woodlot, have to be closed up in winter. I would not have a professional snoop up my chimney with the avowed purpose of fixing the damper, because he would seize the chance to frighten me with all the other things that are wrong in there. *You* will not have to fret about the 90 percent heat loss up your chimney since you will soon have a sufficient supply of wood from your forthcoming slice of forestland. Once the fire is out here, we slap on the plywood facing, or close the door to the room, thereby saving night heat.

In English homes, heavy portieres were once used extensively to cut down on drafts. These wool-lined tapestries were slipped onto brass rods across the doorway and in the hall to seal off a stairwell where there was no door. Adaptations of the practice will, no doubt, again become recherché here in a few years. Insulated curtains have already been warmly received as a means of heat conservation, along with gauche padded window shades that slide down a track.

"wood stove"

Now, about wood stoves. From youngest childhood on, my most secret ambition has been to open all the blocked fireplaces in every unrestored house I have ever visited. This leaves me frantic about the idea that we have to go backward in time and close the operational ones again, to reinstall wood stoves for venting up the flues. Feeding stoves and ranges with the daily ration is a drag and hauling away ashes, dirty work. To some, the wood stove together with kerosene lamps and the kitchen pump, are lingering romantic reminders of genteel Victorian days. I am not fooled by any of this medieval fiction. But, if you have to, put the stoves in according to the best regulations obtainable and the fire department will leave you alone. Otherwise, be ready to entertain them soon after kindling ceremonies.

What more can I say? Weatherstrip all doors and windows. Sleep two or more to a bed with all your animals. Double up on showers to save fuel and go to quilt-making class. You have to help yourself stay warm by bundling up in sweaters and snuggies if you want to be one of the fittest who survives to pass on the hereditary instinct. Stay young and healthy with lower heat and the added benefit of higher humidity, which in the latest findings heightens resistance to respiratory diseases. I have also experienced a tendency toward less new wrinkles and dry skin, plus fewer emerging white strands on my head, maybe.

Wiring

When I was young, I met an old man who had just

"the mice helped him"

rigged up a brilliant light that, with the flick of a switch, would shoot out of a trap in the roof of his attic and illuminate the whole yard if he heard a suspicious noise outdoors in the dark of night. As amazement at his ingenuity turned to talk of wiring and he confessed to re-doing his entire house, I innocently asked him how he got the wire through the walls. He told me that his mice helped him. In retrospect, I realize how fortunate he was to have had mice on his side, as I suspect mine are a lot less cooperative, if not downright malevolent.

Do you have switches that fail to activate your lights, even when treated kindly? My dining room chandelier is controlled by four widely separated switches and, I am beginning to fancy, the aid of an entire phalanx of mini rodents. Perhaps I credit them with too much intelligence. At any rate, if the sequence of switches gets out of whack, nothing, not even sweet talk, will turn those lights on. We have to station four people, one to a switch, and twiddle each at random until the formula is rediscovered. My husband and I are going to be kept running if this condition still prevails when our children leave home.

Wiring is a mystery, and in an old house it is more than confusing. It all seems to miraculously terminate at the junction box which, if you are lucky, has each fuse clearly labeled. Some of our fuses are numbered and indicated on a chart on the box door, but the reference is to rooms named by past occupants. Thus, Granny's sitting room and the mangle (remember that fabulous ironing machine?) now refer to my sewing room and part

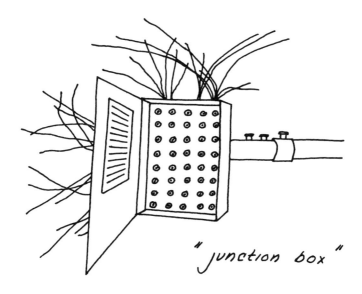

"junction box"

of the cellar. I have managed to keep most of the translations of room names in my head, though the unidentified fuses are tricky, because once I have found out what part of the house they regulate, I invariably forget to note it down.

And then there are the fuses themselves—awful things. Some look dead when they are alive and others look alive when they are dead. My brother who is a fuse expert hesitates to visit me any more because of my penchant for making him look in our junction box to locate a blown fuse before I feed him. Also, if you are not careful when you buy fuses, you may get the wrong thread size, as I have many times. Finally, there are the no-good ones that never get thrown away and are, of course, the first to be chosen as replacements.

I guess it is a good idea to have your wiring checked once in a while. When a switch lights up a dark hall with an overly dynamic spark, something may be wrong. "Bad" wiring has been known to be the cause of many a successful fire and none of us looks forward to that no matter how disillusioned we get with our houses, or how much insurance we have. I have not met an electrician yet, but I think I will have to capitulate one of these days. I hope he does not smoke stinking cigars like my some-time plumber does. So far, I have been able to remove lights that cease to function and can find my way in the dark in most rooms, though I suppose my patience will not last forever.

A possible alternative to rewiring may be the purchase and installation of smoke detectors that are much in vogue today. Mine are so effective, they have a disconcerting way of bleeping when I let a pot in the oven boil over for half a second.

Attic

Once an attic is full, all thoughts of giving up an old house have to be forgotten, as there is no way to either sort out and throw away the accumulation, or move it to another house. A full attic is a sign of stability, roots in a mobile society, and the clue that you are safely entrenched and have overcome all signs of tension about your home. You are at peace.

How long does it take to fill an attic? Ours was full in four years and we would have filled the second one if it

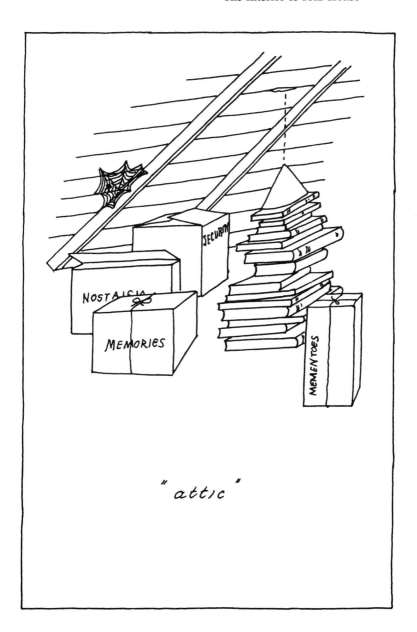

"attic"

had been accessible. (It is too shallow and has to be approached through a small upstairs lavatory by standing on the sink and levitating the rest of the way.) If you have no attic, you should designate a room for that purpose. Your children need the reassurance that when they set up housekeeping, their saved treasures and your rejected furniture will be there to retrieve and put to use. Books too, should be kept and placed in out-of-favor book cases in the attic. When we give a house tour to new friends, we include our attic as it is a source of great appeal for our guests.

Attics are loaded with surprises. You forget what is up there and when you go looking for a lamp or picture frame, you always come across other tempting rejects that had escaped your mind completely. Partly because of his faith in attics and partly for lack of time, upon his mother's death my husband arranged for the removal of his share of her attic to ours, sight unseen. The movers were mystified and unbelieving. They had no way of comprehending the fun we were to have delving into those curious boxes.

Then there is the question of shelter for wild animals. We make the coons stay outdoors, but bats and squirrels and mice all need a roof over their heads in cold weather as much as we do. For a special treat, our cats are allowed in the attic for a good smell, now and again, sometimes to be forgotten until we hear a weak meow.

There are not enough fine things to say about an attic and no one can have a feeling of real permanence in an old house unless his mementoes are carefully stored there, to be pored over at will. Most children know they are cherished and feel a warmth of security if their childhood memories are safe in the attic. It is the only room in our house that my daughter will voluntarily clean, because she is immersed in nostalgia and overcome by love for her home.

By the way, a leak in a raftered attic roof is easy to find since you can see daylight through the crack. One winter day just after a storm when I was foraging in our attic, I found that a neat cone of soft snow had sifted through a small hole onto a pile of books. I looked straight up and sure enough, there was blue sky ahead. A caulking gun and an accurate aim will take care of that perforation when I see it next time.

Cellar

The most rewarding characteristic of a cellar is that it does not need to be dusted regularly. A little sweeping and tidying up occasionally will suffice. Most cellars, while they serve essentially the same purpose as an attic, namely storage, tend to be somewhat rank and hence only appropriate for the less-perishable items. (A cellar is for abandoned goods that you are not quite ready to say goodbye to, whereas an attic is for those things to be saved.) Incidentally, it is never too late to dig a cellar if you do not have one. I know a father who put his boys to work recently, and now they have a splendid new one.

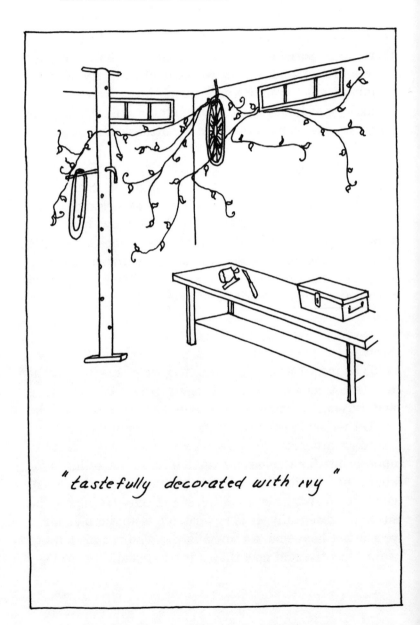

"tastefully decorated with ivy"

Cellars are naturally temperature controlled, cool in summer and moderate in winter. As a measure of humidity, we discovered that out-of-date leather ski boots grow mold with ease in our cellar. If not the place in which to sit reading for any length of time, it is perfect for gentle exercise or puttering in a workshop. My husband has found the atmosphere sufficiently congenial to spend many happy hours (while selectively neglecting the house) rearranging and updating his shop.

Never underestimate the amount of time that can be spent getting ready to do something. There is always the whole shop to be put to rights, missing tools found and others sharpened, and an inventory taken to see what has to be added new. This means many trips to canvass all of his favorite hardware stores (for impulse purchases) with a lumber yard or two sandwiched in between. Then every few weekends, there is the visit to the dump to discard all throwaways and return with whatever the dump has to yield which in turn must be catalogued for fix-up or recycling. The blind is there to, patiently awaiting his inspiration.

Our cellar also has a bicycle repair room tastefully decorated with delicate pale green ivy that grows in from outdoors through invisible cracks in the foundation masonry. This is the place where metal carcasses are saved which, when doled out one at a time, provide an excuse to check out the metal pile at the dump for retrieval of old radios and more bicycle frames to be used for parts or made into bikes and sold. (This is, of necessity, a surreptitious activity. Picking the dump in our town is frowned upon as as infringement on the rights of rats, sea gulls and dump keepers.) My son once had a thriving business in second-hand bikes. This room also housed mini-bikes when in their heyday here, while their motors were being taken apart, studied and sometimes reassembled. The most recent acquisition is bicycle rollers, a new form of self-destruct for our children that enables them to balance their redoubtable racing bikes on cylinders and pedal like mad to go nowhere.

A basement is often necessary to house the aforementioned Lally columns. We have an awesome forest of thirty-five, all sizes and styles, from wide girth trees denuded of bark, to commercial two-by-fours and starkly modern steel tubes. Having gotten accustomed to so many obstacles, we find it possible to manuever without bumping into them too often. Once in a while a two-by-four dislodges, but it is no great hardship to slip it back into place. With plenty of backup support from the rest of the woods, little harm is done. Confidence is ample bracing under your house and by now I think we would be apprehensive without it.

There are, of course, other incidentals in cellars that have the room, such as a furnace, hot-water heater, kitty litter and the wood pile. Strictly speaking, fireplace wood should not be in the cellar. If it is infested with powder post beetles, they can grow weary of their fare and move over to a more succulent part of the house. Since our wood cannot fit in the garage, we do not enjoy trying to burn it

" adversary "

wet. Every time the exterminator comes to spray for this and that throughout the house, he cannot resist telling me that the firewood has to go, and each time, I assure him it is all but on the way out. We figure that one year's supply at a time will not hurt and any damage is unlikely to show up until long after we have gone.

Water seepage into a cellar can be soaked up by whatever is sitting on the floor or it can be controlled by a sump pump. A subterranean cistern that was installed a hundred or more years ago in our cellar used to catch and save precipitation from the roof. Having forgotten that this system is no longer functioning, our cellar has lapses from time to time, and thinks its purpose is still that of collecting water.

We discovered that the gutter downspout at the rear of our house is supposed to fit into a hole in the ground

"wild screaming fight"

which drains the water off toward a defunct cesspool. Once having perfected this connection, we no longer are flooded in that part of the cellar. The opposite side does have some trickle through the stone walls, a condition we have been able to live with.

Cellar windows sometimes surrender to a snowball. One day during a wild meleé featuring hundreds of boys on our front lawn, an icy missile found its way to a small transom window suffering from dry rot, carrying it sash and all into the cellar. The paint was no longer able to hold it together. Several weeks later, my husband managed to close up the gap with a piece of plywood, custom fit. From that day on our cats became more and more restless and jumpy, and I noticed that their dish was empty every morning—a most ominous circumstance. They tried to show me the cellar door and I missed the signals. At the same time the children mentioned hearing loud singing in the kitchen at night. It was not until nearly a week had passed when it slowly dawned on me that, in an effort to seal up the cellar against their feisty feline friends, we had inadvertently entombed an old adversary. When one of the cats complained of a wound, I realized what had been going on and quickly arranged doors and windows so that our unwelcome guest could gracefully escape.

Silver fish

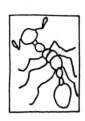
Carpenter ant

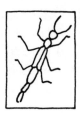
Earwig

Termite

Coleoptera
larvae

Wasp

"Insects"

9. Insects

Now and again, my husband insists that he is kept awake at night by bugs gnawing their way through our house. I protest that he is exaggerating, though the list of insects that salivate at the mere thought of an old house is spectacular.

Ants, the most conspicuous of our visitors, revive with the onset of spring to start their hunt for food. Carpenter ants are the big, black beasts that stop at nothing to get nourishment. While they do not eat wood, they take delight in constructing miles of tunnels through beams to get to their final destination, leaving a fortune in sawdust behind. Multiplying as they march, they work on apple cores and banana peels thoughtlessly thrown into waste baskets, and make quick work of cracker crumbs left over from a furtive midnight snack in bed.

Their kin, the household ants, meanwhile are mopping up in the kitchen. They have a sweet tooth and squeeze through cracks on the way to satisfy their appetites. Mint leaves, thought by some to act as a pesticide for ants, shrivel and curl up on my sink and window sills as those cheeky creatures carefully skirt them.

Moths, if given a chance, are happy to impinge on your hospitality forever. They have been known to inhabit cracks in floors to the exclusion, even, of dust, and are difficult to discourage. When they find themselves shrouded by a wool rug, they exuberantly set to work for months of meals. Unlike many an old house that has a cedar-lined closet designed to thwart these invidious intruders, we have none and to my surprise have also had no trouble with moths, though I have kept up a vigil against them.

Termites cause terror in the hearts of all people. To a termite's mind, an old house is synonymous with rich meals and he has no compunctions about setting to. After all, what business is it of his if the house falls down? Termites have to eat and are solely concerned with survival of the species as they chew up timbers in a quest for more and more wood.

Silverfish thrive on book bindings, cloth and wallpaper. Earwigs are startling to come upon unexpectedly in dark crevices, but they prefer a diet of other small bugs to your household treasures, while wasps are after spiders to bury as food for their young. The pests that would really make you shudder, if you could see them, are classified under Coleoptera. These macabre denizens, the tiny larvae of certain species, feast on beams, carpets, upholstery, furniture and picture frames, to name a few of their wants. They are notorious for their destruction in museums. Fortunately only a restoration artisan can detect evidence of their presence, leaving the rest of us in blissful ignorance unless we make the mistake of inviting an authority into the house. I have had the rear end of one moribund Coleoptera pointed out to me, and prefer to expunge the encounter from my mind.

We came to the conclusion early that an exterminator service might be worth the commitment to its annual fee. An expenditure of several hundred dollars during tenure in a house can, in theory, save thousands in insect carnage. If our man sprays in winter for ants when they are dormant and sets bait for mice in summer when those rascals are off in the fields, well, that's life!

"resident ghost"

10. Night Noises

As a child, I used to lie awake at night in bed in the country, scared half to death by the bark of a fox off in the woods; I remain less than enthusiastic when it comes to the creaks and groans my house emits at night. I still retain an extraordinary ability to imagine that those noises on the other side of my present bedroom door are made by a ghost. If, for some reason, I fail to latch my door at night and only push it to, an hour later when I am snug in bed immersed in a book, to my horror the door will jump back with a loud and shattering report. I have difficulty adjusting to this violence.

Intellectually, I understand that most night noises in an old house are no more than timbers contracting as they cool after the heat of the day. Or, perhaps the house is lamenting a rising wind. Although it is not just in novels that the wind "whistles" around a house, swinging the garden gate or brushing a branch against your casement window, there definitely are noises in my home that I cannot account for. I have often heard footsteps in the upstairs hall, what I could swear sounded like calculated movement, only to find nothing there when I had the courage to look out.

A certain number of sounds in a house are easily verifiable. Domestic quarrels among busy mice nesting in a wall are frequently accompanied by little shrieks and sometimes the entire coterie can be heard in rapid descent from ceiling level to the floor or beyond. Cats and dogs can stealthily dislodge crockery from a shelf or china closet that will crash to the floor, sending echoes throughout a still house. I am even willing to believe that objects can fall unaided from a crowded cabinet when they have been jiggled, over time, too close to the edge.

Having ruled out a phantom as the perpetrator of unexplained night noises in my house, I do know of a household that is unable to be so glib as they sheepishly admit to having a resident ghost. Although I have an ongoing hate/love relationship with the idea of a ghost I can call my own, I feel a little jealous that they have someone to blame for all untoward midnight chaos in their home. Without visible manifestation of such a scapegoat, I am forced to search elsewhere for causes of my own nighttime din. Still, while I think that they are rational and sane people, I can always fall back, if pressed, on the notion that they have overdone it. The owners of a house that is haunted, on the other hand, have a rare opportunity to make the acquaintance of their strange bedfellow and write a best-seller.

The thought that all night noises are not a direct result of a relaxing house or click of the thermostat (an overture to heat flow) may keep you awake at night sleuthing. I find that I alternate between being immobilized by fear and being too much of a skeptic to check out all bangs and whimpers. I am not above poking my husband alive to make him investigate, however, in times of indecisive agitation. I try to limit this course of action, though, because I have been embarrassed too many times. Once, what I was certain was a burglar walking along the back balcony of one house we lived in, turned out to be large, damp leaves rhythmically dropping onto the boards.

Night noises are disturbing whether you know their origin or not, but they should not be allowed to crystallize any decision to move. There is no guarantee that your next place would be any quieter. Also, I am beginning to think that it takes a certain level of psychic development to be aware of a ghost in a house and since I may have one at present that I cannot perceive or sense, it might be worthwhile to cultivate that elevated achievement. The noise with no explanation would be much more rewarding if you could pin it on a wandering spirit. A state of heightened sensory awareness is a highly desirable goal among large parts of today's population, and you might not wish to be left behind.

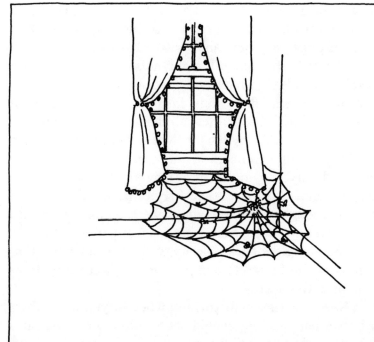

"a friend"

11. Hints on Housekeeping

KEEPING HOUSE in an old edifice bears little resemblance to the same exercise in a new one. In fact, if you do not crave a model home, it is much easier. An old house that is immaculate and dust free might as well be new with less work for the house cleaner. I find that mine is impossible to keep clean, so I enjoy the faintly murky effect that simulates greater age. You cannot always be apologizing for the lack of cleanliness or tidiness in your home, because you will simply bore your friends and acquaintances to death. My husband and I feel safe in saying that ours is "a festering atmosphere of creativity," a catch phrase that to our minds gently explains away the turbulence of our habitat.

It is true that people will always notice if your house is messy or dirty, yet they will never appreciate any amount of improvements you make. For that reason, I find that if I am unconcerned, others fall into line. Perhaps you have to decide whether your house is for living or just for show. Personally, while I like to look at pictures of sterile houses, I have decided that I want my house to be home to my children and their friends and our pets. Under these circumstances, the lived-in look is natural, almost to a fare-thee-well, but I have made my peace and thrive on the noise and companionship.

Wall-to-wall carpeting in an old house is out. Not only is it usually inappropriate, it is too easily stained. The one reason to use it is when there has been in the past a matting on the floor. This was a covering of coarsely woven, straw rugging that was nailed down around the edges of the room and if your floors have been sanded and refinished, the holes will still be there as a reminder. In a pickle like this, when you choose to re-cover a floor, stick with gravy-colored carpeting.

Oriental rugs, no matter how worn (actually, thread-bare ones are a symbol of reverse snobbery), are the most practical because they do not show spills. Used with a rug pad, squeaks are elegantly muffled. Painted floors show the dust, even after vacuuming, enabling you to make a real difference by running a damp mop over them for more formal affairs.

I have recently come to grips with the problem of regular transference into the kitchen (via deeply ridged boot soles) of a large portion of our dirt driveway. I admitted to myself that I am no longer titillated by seeing

110

how much dirt and stones I can amass in my daily sweeping. It seems that a paved driveway is in order if I can be assured that it will not look like a parking lot and my husband agrees to part with the colossal sum of money the project will require.

Finger prints on walls and woodwork bother some people, but truthfully, if you are busy, you will not see them. One day not long ago I was visiting a relative who complained of the amount of time she had spent washing away finger prints, and I thought to myself, "Goodness, do people still do that?" With an active and meaningful life, such trivia are soon forgotten.

Spider webs belong in the same category, I suppose, except that spiders are do-gooders and voraciously trap and devour all the beetles, flies, carpenter ants and wasps they can get their hands on. With strategically located webs, an annoying fly buzzing in your house will soon make that fatal mistake and stumble into one, saving you the trouble of trying to swat it. These friends tend to gravitate inside during the late fall in search of comfort and protection and have a period of intense activity as winter closes in. This coincides with those unexpected, late warm days when screens are off windows and yet it is tempting to open them for the last of the clean fresh air.

Washing windows, especially if yours are numerous, is a thankless chore. Unless you are compulsive about it, just wash the ones your eye catches daily and dispense with the rest. When I was a teenager, I used to clean house in the spring for an aged great-aunt. She made me wrap my rag around a two-inch wooden peg to get into all the corners of her hundreds of tiny panes. That is probably why I presently find I have better things to do with my time.

When I tired of the spartan Shaker look, I outfitted my whole house with cotton ball-fringe curtains, only to learn later that the same style was available in dacron. I now regret all the ironing I have to do, if I tackle them at all. Dacron costs more, but the savings in labor is dramatic and there are many varieties to suit every architectural era.

The single most irksome challenge in an old house is dust. Anyone who cannot live with dust is defeated from the beginning. On the other hand, if you feel as I do, that a thin veneer augments the charm and authenticity of antique furniture and accessories, then life is more joyful. If someone happens to admire a trinket that has a liberal frosting of dust on it, I hasten to explain that I did not want to disturb its old-world look. I confess, however, that I do take dust rag in hand, from time to time, and run over the most obvious surfaces—otherwise we would be buried in no time, as the residue regularly recirculates through the hot air system. But it is not possible to keep an old house shining without continual attention, and that is basically unproductive.

Selective neglect demands that you move as the spirit dictates, allowing freedom to function in less than ideal conditions most of the time. Shun the impulse to clean when you think you should, simply keep it in mind

until you are ready. I find that dinner parties sprinkled throughout the year give me just the stimulation I need to clean house, and I am able to be reasonably carefree in between.

Family members who are collectors and never throw away a thing are considered by some as incorrigible. Not so; they are only building their own nests of permanence. If you can accept this fact from the start, you will select a house with closet space to spare. Also, bookcases for books, magazines, papers and puzzles, can fit into many an odd corner.

Our children take after their parents and learned early the pleasurable art of saving. It might be said that approval of this demeanor condones the postponement of decision-making. However, that is not the case as the decision has already been made and it is firm. The need to save is solid and basic, and irreversible psychological damage can result from forcing a collector to divest himself of any of his trove. This does not mean that one of us might not give up whole portions, now and again. After all, what is of vital importance today is not necessarily so later.

This then, is a warning to those who would use a heavy hand when cleaning their children's or spouse's rooms. I have learned that by working with my family instead of against them we gain mutual respect for each other when I am sympathetic to their needs. I do not ask them to throw out that which is a part of them. Certain piles can safely be packaged for storage, while others are organized, but kept in place for the time being. When the floor is found, it can be vacuumed and as window sills and desk tops are revealed, they too can be washed and we are all content.

Most housekeeping can be broken down to two major tasks: picking up and cleaning. It can be helpful to have a cleaning lady, though I found from the small amount of experience with them when our children were babies that I was still forced to do half the job. Picking up and putting away was almost as much of an effort for me as the whole job would have been. Then there was the problem of personal involvement with their private lives. Either they became so possessive with my house that there was no way I could get an idea in edgewise, or they had unsolvable troubles at home that I got inextricably woven into. In the end I was so caught up with their pain and sorrows that I felt guilt over happenings that had nothing to do with me. In my generosity, I would soon be letting them off early each week, loaded down with food and second-hand clothing. And, of course, if the quality of their performance declined, I did not have the heart to fire them. I finally gave up as they tended to snicker at older houses, anyway, disliking the extra work they made, and I missed having full charge of my own domain. The ideal housekeeper has found a place for everything, and everything is in its place. This is unquestionably a salubrious way to live. I have never been able to come close. Our kitchen is a perfect example of the shortcomings of an old house, as well as my own frailty.

"<u>MY</u> kitchen table!"

The table is the focal point of our kitchen and a repository for everything from school books to tools. Everyone who passes through drops what he or she is holding onto the table and I must put it away, or find a new place for it. I generally first stow upstairs goods on the back stairs in the hope that their owners will grab them on the way up. But, in the final analysis, as we thread our way past the piles, when my optimism flags and broad hints offer no help, I take them up myself.

Magazines are especially menacing. Although we save as many as we can, they cannot all stay, and yet if I throw one away, it will be in demand the next day. Newspapers too stack up around our ears. I have, however, learned the nifty trick of stuffing them into the

116

weekly supply of grocery bags (that I did not know what to do with) for recycling. Tools and other strange bits of hardware are another source of frustration, but I have found a solution. I like to keep my own hammer, screw drivers, pair of pliers, screws, nails and so forth in the cabinet under the sink. These implements, so universally in demand, are never there when I need them, so I have adopted the practice of expropriating replacements from the kitchen table.

My counter, what little there is of it, is also painfully open to the spillover from the table and I often find my working area reduced to a useless one-foot square. When I parcel out what has collected on the counter to passers-by, they put it on the table and disappear.

I have given up buying small appliances. They all require counter space which I ran out of long ago, and I refuse to keep putting them in a closet and getting them out again each time they are used. This does have the advantage of saving money, a benefit no one can argue with. At the moment, I am in a marathon argument with one of my sons about the desirability of purchasing an electric popcorn popper. His is a low pressure, if unremitting, approach, and I am hoping the urgency will pass until he leaves home.

The laundry is another scourge, largely because it is full of jackets, sweatshirts, socks and underwear that belong to children other than my own. When a cool day turns warm, they dash home to dinner minus a jacket only to return the next day wearing a new one. On rainy

"back stairs"

days, they strip to borrow dry clothes from my gang and leave their outfits in the dryer. They are too self-conscious to claim underwear even if the name is on the wasteband, though if I make a concerted effort, I can send home a bagful of the remainder now and again. Sometimes my tribe will be attracted to a pair of socks or a sweatshirt, reducing the stack.

The reason for this discourse about my kitchen and environs is that it illustrates the generic defects of old kitchens—not enough closets, empty walls or shelves. Although I think mine was built on for the purpose, it was done in the days when summer kitchens provided on entry way with a place for boots and a coat-hanging hall. The pantry which is now a lavatory held all the pots and pans and dishes. And, in the old days, there was no large refrigerator and dishwasher to take up room.

With four doors, four windows and all the necessary gadgetry protruding from walls plus added closets and the laundry, my kitchen is much smaller than it was originally, and not as convenient as a modern one in a new house. Another consideration is the kitchen table which uses up what little room there is left over. In a more formal era, all meals were eaten in the dining room. While we could do that, it represents more work and we enjoy the ease of handing food from the stove to the table. We also like to sit at the table and chat at any time of day. It has become a famous gathering place where our children and their friends solve the problems of their teenage world.

119

"famous monogram"

12. Remodeling and the Budget

MUCH has been written on the subject of remodeling an old house and if we take it all to heart there is hardly anything we are allowed to do. In one breath "they" disparage the restoration of your house to its original period and in the next, you must retain the old-time kitchen. It seems to me that the state of your pocketbook and the dictates of the house after you have settled in will soon suggest what to do and how to do it.

If you spend all your discretionary funds on making the inside (and the outside) of your home exemplary at once, you may not have any money left over for furnishings. I have seen ambition of this kind; the houses are stately and bleak. You can, on the other hand, re-do one room at a time. It is more difficult when you have to move furniture, but the likelihood of making mistakes is lessened and you can keep enough money in the checking account to buy an antique once in a while when you want to. Antique furniture may have been what you carved your initials on as a child, though today it doubles in value over night. (My husband, as a young hellion, decorated his mother's Sheraton chest of drawers with his famous monogram.)

I frankly see no harm in stripping away later decor that was added to update a building. A stamped metal ceiling in a Colonial house may not please your eye. Take it down. "Gingerbread" inside and out that clashes with your style can be eliminated with minimum fuss. Still, on the other side of this issue, I could never be talked into removing my large windows to return to a dark house, though if I had to, I would not hesitate to replace big panes with smaller ones.

Comfort in your old house has to have priority and for that reason I am for a modern kitchen, no matter how incongruous it may appear. After all, a goodly amount of any housewife's day is spent in the kitchen, so why put up with antediluvian devices? Rip it out and put in the most sumptuous kitchen you can afford, but for goodness' sake save the old fireplace and accoutrements.

When you remodel, think about inserting a time capsule into a wall for the delight of the next owners of the house to make a change. We have filled up so many pockets, I cannot recall where they all are. A few pages from a Sears catalogue, an antique gimcrack and a coin or two will be acceptable to anyone finding them.

Some houses still have the cast-iron kitchen range extant. The darling of today's energy conservationists, they are worth money, and unless you were brought up with one as I was, you may find them camp enough to revitalize and put to use. There are those who claim that a stew never tasted as good as when it simmered all day on the back of a wood stove.

Not many years ago it was considered a waste of space and the massive kitchen fireplace to keep an old kitchen alive in a restoration. Instead, it was made into the living room. Now, however, there is more of a trend back toward family gatherings in and around the kitchen and the closing off of other downstairs rooms in winter to save fuel. The family room concept so popular in new houses has revived the Colonial habit of action around the flaming hearth, an idea you might want to contemplate when pondering kitchen possibilities in your home.

Seriously weigh the removal of walls if your house is

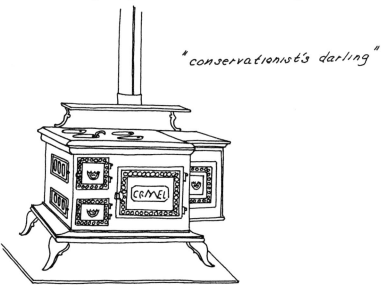

"conservationist's darling"

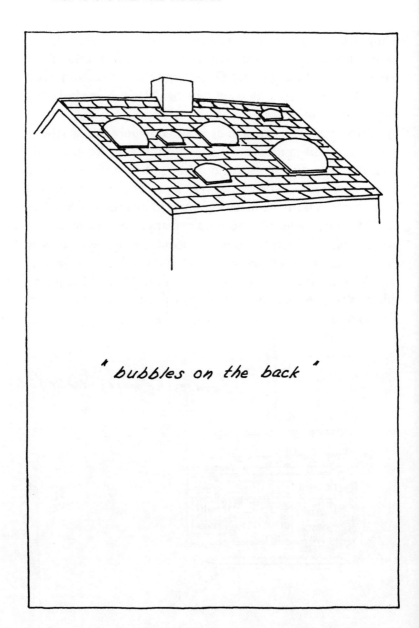

a jumble of crabbed rooms. Beware only of the need for beam support. Past occupants ruthlessly divided large rooms into two for more bedrooms or to make a hallway separate from the living room. Often it is possible to attain the feeling of sweeping spaciousness and relieve cramped quarters. Mercy, some folks must have felt that every room needed a door to close out the world and hide behind back in the days when all windows were equipped with dark green shades habitually pulled down to half mast.

Do you really want to take those layers of paint off your exposed beams? It is an unbelievable amount of work and they will not look right if cracks and depressions retain even a trace of light-colored paint. Remember our forefathers have used paint liberally since the 1700s. And dormers in the roof out front? Try to be sensitive about the appearance of your house. If you need more light, put some bubbles on the back; they are practical and very chic. When you need to add another bathroom, plan it with care. I have seen huge converted bedrooms which left you seated by the window miles away from the door that you forgot to lock. In other words, do not be afraid of making improvements, just use a little common sense about the final result.

The do-it-yourself craze is upon us and while I pretend to disparage skill at heftier tasks, a considerable amount of cash can be saved by learning to paint and wallpaper your own home. Wallpapering is easy and with a little practice, a novice can turn professional after

"learn to wallpaper"

completing one room. Unfortunately, I have done so much home decorating that I am bored with it and have several unfinished projects—an evil to dodge. Nonetheless, do not feel that you should give up all pursuits to be a slave to your home. Wallpaper or paint when you want to but save time for yourself too.

You may have noticed an effect which I find curious and intriguing. As you drive or walk along a village street at night and pass homes that are lit up for evening activities, you will observe that some of them appear warm and inviting, while others seem forbidding and cold. I think this must have to do with the aura created by furniture, rugs, curtains and woodwork inside and perhaps with the tint of lamp shades. This is not an issue of great moment, it merely illustrates the intangibility of nuance inherent in the choice of color, pattern and texture, a selection that bears heavily on the look of a house illuminated at night, and might mirror too the personality of the decorator who lives inside. What does your house look like from the outside at night?

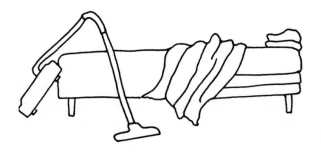

"suggestively leaning"

13. Getting Ready for the Party

THE THRILL of giving a dinner party is surpassed only by the excitement of preparations beforehand. In my family, everyone participates whether he or she joins the party or not, because that is my way of cleaning house. Since the house has been allowed to coast for the past month or so (try two months?) there is abundant opportunity for each member to show his stuff.

Normally, if our soiree is to be on a Saturday, I try to do some cleaning every day during the preceding week. First, I haul out the vacuum and work my way through the ground-floor rooms and up the stairs. That is usually enough effort for one day; I am not used to the agony of so much tiresome physical exertion. The second day I manage to do the upstairs until I reach the children's bedrooms where I suggestively leave the vacuum leaning against a bed. My boys are just as clever at stepping over a vacuum without seeing it as they are at winding through heaps decorating the back stairs.

Next, I straighten up my share of the house and do a little dusting. It is against my principles to dust higher than I can see on the premise that most wives are no taller than I. If my husband complains, I hand him the cloth. Sometimes I polish a piece of silver or brass to catch my guests' attention and divert their gaze from other furnishings that may look shabby. I try to wash the kitchen floor once or twice a year whether it needs it or not and then there are bathrooms and the kitchen stove to clean.

By Saturday morning I have to start cooking and remind the children that I expect their rooms to pass inspection by evening, in case we want to show off the house. And then my husband springs into action. He invariably starts in his office and when that is neat, he decides to wash and wax the floor, a performance that more often than not extends through to my sewing room, space I secretly know he has his eye on as potential for expanding his office. This is all well and good except that he is apt to get his hands on the Lestoil and when he has finished his own quarters, he wanders by, bucket in hand, swiping chair rails on the way to find other places to scrub. If he attacks the stairs, that will remind him to go up, and by the end of several hours, the house is thick with Lestoil fumes and I am afraid we will all be asphyxiated before our guests even arrive. (The last time

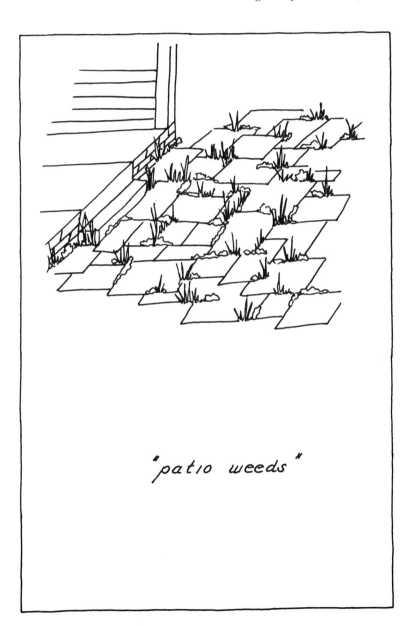

"patio weeds"

this happened, there were other chores I was depending on his doing for me, such as laying a fire in the living room fireplace. When I went off to rescue him, I found that he had bribed the boys to help him shuffle a large chest from our "glory hole" into his dressing room, a move he had vaguely considered for months.) In the meantime, my daughter comes to and begins on her room, a full day's work which she has left for the last two hours.

The outside has to be spruced up sometimes, as well. In early spring the children (under duress) gather twigs and branches from the lawn. Summer means the lawn has to be mowed and in fall, the toughest season for us, leaves are raked and hauled away. Occasionally we also rake up paint chips from around the more accessible foundations of the house so that we do not look too nonchalant. The patio flagstones have to be weeded from time to time and after warm weather is well established in spring, spent bird seed must be shoveled up and moved out, if we plan to entertain outdoors. A final inspection inside shoves clothes into drawers and retrieves books and magazines from the floor around beds.

A crescendo is reached late in the afternoon when the phone begins to ring and the children lay escape plans with their friends. One call adds to another as the vacuum whines upstairs and I am trying to overcome Lestoil toxemia and put final touches on the meal. By this time my husband is likely to be in the cellar, having forgotten he is after firewood, intently sawing up boards to build himself a Shaker cabinet. If we ever do finish our preparations, it is to descend upon the one bathroom in the house that we all seem to have to use, everyone demanding a shower at once.

The truth is, we are usually ready on time and sit around waiting while our guests are late. Nevertheless, when they finally arrive, the food is always delicious, conversations scintillating and, if the cats do not get overexcited with the advent of new faces in the house and woof up their dinners, everyone enjoys a delightful evening.

There is also the added satisfaction of a clean house and the relief that it will not have to be done again for a while and we can go about the more important business of living in our old house.

"lecherous tattletale"

14. Sex in the Old House

It SEEMS expedient to put some sex in this effort to attract the reader who has come to expect sensationalism in every book he picks up. I do this purely as a diversionary tactic for the purpose of pepping up the otherwise rather dry and sobering content here. I also feel the need to mollify my husband, who complains that I never get enough sex in my writing and will probably doubt its applicability now.

Once again we have to look to our ancestors for light on the subject. The Puritan position was not only comforting, but foolproof. Theirs was a method that assured the prolific expansion of a family that worked on and improved our houses. The bundling board, far from being the primitive form of birth control we have always assumed it to be, had a knot hole in it. And, any claim that an unmarried couple who went to bed together was fully clothed is quickly exposed as a myth upon a cursory reading of court records of the time. Many a hapless pair was caught red-handed by a lecherous tattletale who peeked through the cracks in the floor overhead, generating a strong incentive to lay down a new top layer of boards. Illegitimate children abounded in those days. Young maids, bored and overworked, were susceptible to indecent proposals from the vigorous youth, allowing them to steal kisses and their chastity. This age group had no need for aphrodisiacs.

Yes, they had it "all together" and we should consider ourselves fortunate to have the legacy of so many large and comfortable homes today. Our houses grew to accommodate the average family of a dozen or more children, all of whom were expected to work to help the improvement and growth of the estate.

Since a multi-generational family was the rule, many small bedrooms were provided upstairs to oblige copulating couples of all ages. The cord in the rope beds was kept well oiled to avoid disturbing those more interested in sleep. Next to the long dark kitchen in the back of the house was the keeping room, still there in many homes. This was held in reserve for birthing and the ill because it was beside the warmest room in the house that had a fire in the hearth all day long. It may have played its part in conception as well, when everyone else had gone to meeting.

The earthy quality of the Puritans, not limited to the

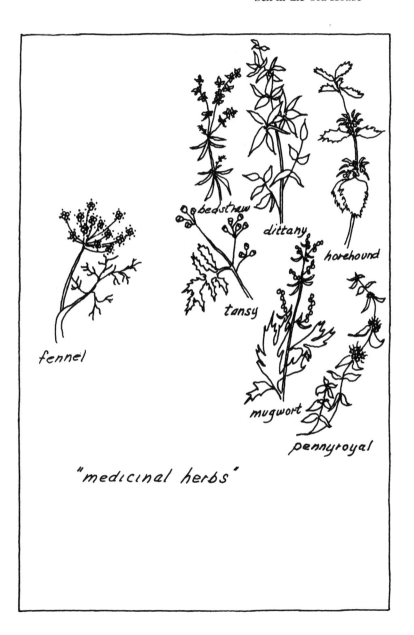

fennel

bedstraw

dittany

horehound

tansy

mugwort

pennyroyal

"medicinal herbs"

early settlers, was characteristic too of the Victorians who hid under a defensive posture of dignity and false disinterest. Herb gardens, some vestiges of which we have inherited, were planted and prospered early, to be revived and appreciated by the Victorians not for the beauty of the blossoms but for the so-called medicinal value of the herbs themselves.

As an aid in childbirth, there were basil, dittany, horehound, and mugwort. To help breed milk in mothers, they grew dill, fennel and lettuce. Fennel, mullein, and pennyroyal helped bring on "the term." And for the listless, to stir up lust, bedstraw, nettles boiled in white wine, southern wood and valerian did the job wonderfully well. To prevent pregnancy, they used mint and tansy. Knot grass stopped gonorrhea and lettuce took away the ill effects of drunkenness.* Without the need for drying sheds and lofts for the myriad harvest of herbs, our attics would not have been finished and floored and other rooms tight and dry.

Drinking and sex have always been linked and hence the large cellars we enjoy today. Storage for hogsheads of beer and wine and later nineteenth-century "medicines," has since become quite handy for workshops and bicycle repair rooms. Much time and care went into the making of beer, and cider was not fit to drink until it was hard. The cider was served at every meal, traditionally set out on the table by the youngest child, and a jug was provided

* George Francis Dow, *Everyday Life in the Massachusetts Bay Colony,* Boston, 1935.

in the fields to pass around freely at the end of each row. There were times when the "simple" girl who took lunch in a basket out to the men was late for dinner that night. Roundly scolded, she was not swayed from further gratifying her appetite for a more prolonged dalliance in the woods beyond with the lad of her choice at the next earliest opportunity. The Victorians also were notorious for concealing a bottle in the barn or cellar to visit for the occasional swig. And why not? Cook was nipping in the kitchen.

So you see, our dwellings have been the bemused witnesses to plenty of "goings on." Tumbling in the clover and husking bees, not to mention secret trysts in the best upstairs bedchamber, all manifestations of more than a passing interest in sex, have had a radical and profound effect upon our homes.

"imagined old crone"

15. The Old Folks at Home

OLD HOUSES and old folks go together. Hardly a Thanksgiving has rolled around that we have not thought of going over the river and through the woods to grandmother's house. And you have to believe that her house was old. Most grandparents that are still dug into their homes want to stay there until the day they are gathered to their maker. In an age when too many of our elderly are considered excess baggage and their children want to see the burden of care shifted to other shoulders, I have some special ideas on how you can stay at home where you belong.

The theory of selective neglect was fabricated by and for oldsters who, after a lifetime of surviving in their old places, have learned to take tribulations in stride and have developed the cunning required to be independent.

You know the vultures are out there flying around your old house, hoping you will die or become feeble and have to be moved out, so they can swoop in and buy your house for a song and fix up the dilapidated old treasure. If "they" are not young couples who come by to butter you up, wantonly, they are the local realtors who have had an eye on your place for a long time, waiting to pounce. I know an old woman who was adroitly conned into signing over her house and all of her possessions to a wily scoundrel who was not even remotely related to her. As part of the deal she was to have the use of half the place until she died and then everything would become his. She had no progeny, but there were distant relatives who felt that ancestral portraits (she had many) and heirlooms should have remained in the family instead of passing into the hands of a stranger who was up to no good. There was no recourse when the dirty deed was done—a time-old swindle, too often successful.

To remain in your home you have to strike an ingenious balance between being self-sufficient, and asking for a little help now and then. You should abstain from being a burden on your children and yet you want to think up an excuse to see them once in a while. When you play your cards right, if you are poor, the mere suggestion that you would be forced to sell an antique tilt-top table might bring them to paint the house for you, because they would rather inherit that piece than lose it altogether. If you are rich they may want to clean your chimney to be able to come into more money later on. Ingratiate your-

"she baked beans"

self by cooking lavish delectable meals and tell gripping stories of the past while they are there.

In order to keep down your property tax, refrain from trying to maintain your old house in flawless condition. Even with tax abatement for the elderly your share can be a financial drain. You will not be expected to sustain a showplace, anyway. Old people are traditionally supposed to live in mysterious, overgrown houses that evoke inscrutable secrets. My mother lives alone and although there is nothing unusual looking about her house, the children in the area decided among themselves that she was a witch. One of those alarmists was quite surprised to find when he screwed up his courage to visit her that she was a delightful lady and fun to talk to, not at all the old crone they had conjured up.

Of course you have to keep your wits about you if you plan to stay secure in your old home. One slip and there will be cause for worry and you might be hustled out in a hurry. My great-aunt Mabel who was dubbed "unstable Mabel" by my cousin took to baking beans on a regular basis for the imminent arrival of her mother for a visit. Her mother had been dead for thirty years.

Hold on to familiar surroundings to stay alert and young and because our most spirited neighborhoods are a mixture of young and old. Children and teenagers whose grandparents live far away need old folks around to be exposed to and become acquainted with, so they can learn to know and like them. Their parents want to help you; will protect your home when you are out, plow your driveway in winter and enjoy doing those extras to have the pleasure of your company. Transportation for the elderly, home-health aides and meals-on-wheels are all trying to say, "We want you to remain where you are in the intimacy of your home where you can be free and have more autonomy."

So shut the door on that crafty antiques man who tries to get you to sell your furniture for little or nothing. Hold on to everything you have so it will seem like a hopelessly difficult mess to sort out. Your children will be less apt to insist on a move to a small apartment or nursing home when they consider the work ahead of them. And try to make sense, even if you feel your mind is wandering. When you see the leaves piling up under the dining room table on a fall day, like my grandfather did while he was sitting there with all the windows closed and the shades half drawn, pretend they are not there and act as if life is going on as usual. Good luck and many happy returns of the day!

"A famous gourmet restaurant"

16. Strategic Commercial Prestige

No BOOK can be considered complete without presentation of the flip side. When all is said and done there remains the old house (like our unwanted elderly) that has been caught up in the midst of social progress under the name of urban sprawl. A noteworthy and salvageable veteran in the heart of a small country town or on the fringe of a burgeoning suburban center deserves the respect given anything that has proven tried and true, has suffered and held up over the ages. The self-esteem of this old house can be saved and nurtured for many years to come. Various societies and trusts have been set up today for exactly that purpose—the preservation of our national heritage of aged and significant buildings.

This is what to do: Buy an old charmer that is so close

to downtown that no one wants to live there. Move in upstairs and convert the first floor into a famous gourmet restaurant. The initial cost may be high because the land in a growing town will, in all probability, be regarded as of more value than the structure. Be sure to apply for the requisite permits and if the land is not zoned commercial have that guarantee in pocket before you commit your and the bank's cash. In an area where restaurants are scarce and employees from businesses in the surrounding region pour into town for lunch, you should have a smashing success.

Few can resist the combination of an historic house, in as natural a setting as you can create, and fine food. An ingenuous atmosphere, domestic and intimate with small rooms, cozy groupings, Colonial decor and a congenial bar, is eternally seductive for those who want to escape to a homelike glow, away from home. You will especially draw upon the tired shopkeeper who longs to hide away in calm and obscurity for an unhurried drink after being trod on by the public all day, and before he goes home to the turbulent realities of wife and children. He is sure to become your friend and confessor, as well as a regular patron at both the bar and in the dining room. When he has introduced his associates and salespersons, they too are bound to bring in all their personal and business contacts. Noontime crowds made up of non-brownbaggers flock to savor a tasty well-served lunch, and businessmen are celebrated for lingering over important deals, happy to consummate them under your very nose.

"consummated business"

The wholesome juxtaposition of a comfortable home aloft and thriving business below is economic and spares the daily commute to work. When you want to expand, space is already available and you can move out to more luxurious quarters. The reason I suggest a restaurant is that in summer you can attract the tourist trade. A tourist is always hoping to find sustenance in the desiccated historical houses he has come to tour. Far from offering what he craves, those ancient inns and taverns have served up nothing but anecdotes for years and swept away the last crumb so long ago no one can remember when. Weary, hot, thirsty and hungry, his appeal falls on deaf ears. The timeless tavern down the street from me has had dozens of phone calls over the years from people trying to make reservations for dinner, and has even had

149

crazies bang on the door to let them in for drinks in a tap room that ceased to function more than a hundred years ago. Yours could be the best of all possible worlds, an antiquated interior to peruse, plus the oasis for exhausted travelers.

You do not want to run a restaurant? How about dishing out books instead? Start with new ones and work up to the old and rare. Books can be handsomely arranged in period rooms. Sprinkle around an antique settee, some trunks and a grandfather's clock to help patrons feel at ease as they browse. The family will be nearby to thwart vandalism and see that the roof is free from leaks. Books are allergic to neglected roofs and many an absentee landlord cares little when his tenant's livelihood is threatened by water damage.

The country has proved a powerful lure to many city dwellers tired of the competitive corporate rat race and living in expensive high-rise apartments that have no attics or cellars for their collections. A recent trend of mass migration from the city is proof that frazzled businessmen would rather settle for the double jeopardy of an old house and a risky new enterprise away from the hurly-burly. This is not the same as the retirement of older folks to the country, as a living still has to be made and the simplicity of small-town life a necessity to assuage ragged nerves.

If books are not your line, try women's or men's clothing, bicycles, fabric, antiques or anything that is merchandizable. Whatever the opportunity, you will be safely ensconced in a magic milieu and nearly all costs can be charged off as business expenses on your income tax. All of this may sound a little crass, but do not overlook the grim prospect of that old house being carelessly torn down to make way for a parking lot, or a nondescript new professional building. It happens every day and broken hearts are soon forgotten. So join the effort to save our history and do yourself a favor in the bargain. You will be honored and feted for caring.

"broken hearts are soon forgotten"

"polished hot water heater"

17. Postscript: How to Get Rid of Your Old House

I F YOU can not give it away, then you must sell it. Selling an old house, after learning to live with its idiosyncracies by following the soothing wisdom of this book or from your own edifying experience, is akin to the betrayal of a personal confidante. Like Scarlet, try to put off thinking about it until tomorrow. (Maybe you could move the house to your new destination.) When that tomorrow dawns, however, your departure should not be born of desperation as much as characterized by a melancholy wrench from the safe haven you have grown to love and understand.

No house is perfect, so you should feel that yours is as desirable as any other on the market, after the work you have put into it and the affection you have given it. Undoubtedly, all those people who wanted to buy it while you were living there, with no intention of selling, will rally to the fore. They have just been hiding in the woodwork, waiting.

Arrange for tours in good weather, if possible, so that a roof leak will not be in evidence and your windows will not need to be washed if you stick to evening hours. Winter is a good time to begin, when there is snow covering the roof and hiding foundations. Crab grass and dandelions will be dormant along with the rest of the lawn, and overgrown shrubs nipped back by frost.

Prevent the irreparable error of breathing the minutest sigh of relief that you are about to unload a white elephant. Mistaken assumptions would be made on the other side and even the mildest joke, if misinterpreted, could spell disaster. It is awful to get started on a false note with either realtor or buyer and makes it almost impossible to reverse the trend.

When you put a high price tag on the house, you do not seem in a hurry to sell and the owner naturally feels it is worth more than everyone else's. Also, you want to be able to settle for a much lower bid to produce the appearance of giving in to a steal. With realistic expectations, on the other hand, there will be fewer questions asked and less hemming and hawing and you might conclude the deal faster.

Your preparations for sale should embrace taking all the blinds to the dump, once and for all. Honestly, why not spare the next owners? I think I would also paint the Lally columns in the cellar to make them more pleasing.

"take blinds to the dump"

First impressions are terribly important and you want to avoid any hint that there is much to be done before a new owner moves in. And too, try to avert suspicion that you can no longer afford to live there because it costs too much to maintain.

As tentative buyers show up for a tour, size them up quickly and respond in kind. Cheer the glum ones, calm those who are nervous or tense and tease the enthusiastic. If they are after a big house, count the baths and closet dressing room into the measure. For a smaller size requirement, leave off bathrooms and the kitchen, mentioning that the ceilings are low, making everything more compact and snug. For wealthier prospects, the grounds are elegant or the potential is there, and for tighter budgets, the yard and greenery are easy care. The ghost zealot will be rewarded with strange noises indeed, otherwise there definitely are no ghosts.

I would insist on staying in the house until it is sold and the mortgage obtained, because a furnished house is much more enticing than an empty one. Vacant places are spooky and unfulfilling. The lingering essence of dispersed families is confusing and indefinable, creating an elusive gloom or freakish quality too enigmatic to unravel.

Do what you have to inside to get ready for the press of buyers and local snoops, townsfolks who will simply be lookers out of curiosity. Lift up the edges of rugs to paint over scuffed floors and vacuum the ceilings often. Pull down shades and close the door to the children's room and call it a supplemental attic. I cannot imagine what I would do with my boys' rooms. The cellar will have to be swept out and anything sold to new owners can be discounted from your moving bill. Consider polishing the hot-water heater to make it look new and maybe dust the furnace too. You might turn off the master valves to leaking faucets and running toilets during visiting hours to make them less distracting; and whatever else you do, keep smiling.

Now is the time for a big garage sale, with a few near-antiques included to attract a large crowd. If the attic is still full, add some of that. I recently heard of a man who backed a truck up to his third story and just threw the stuff out the window. Not a bad idea. Anything goes in a garage sale. Malfunctioning lawn mowers and motor tools do well. For many years my sons and their father loved picking up motorized gadgets that were dead, but showed promise.

Real estate agents have a sedate businesslike approach to selling houses and will try to transform you into a preconceived model of predictable behavior. They do not want you there during "Open House" on a Sunday, being pleasant to possible buyers going through. They are afraid you will leave a soiled coffee cup in the kitchen sink, or otherwise give the impression that someone lives in the house. They are especially fearful that you will break down and start some uncontrollable sentimental ranting about how wonderful your home is. So stay out of the way, particularly if there is dickering over the price, lest in a fit of generosity, you undermine your own best interests.

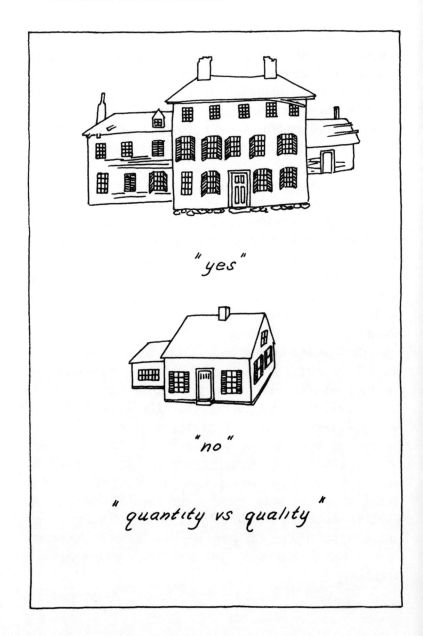

I try not to think about moving from our house, since every inch of available space is full, and my cats would never agree to being parted from their friends. Besides, my husband and I disagree as to where we would go. His fantasy is that of getting the old house experience behind him to close off an era, whereas I think only in terms of buying a smaller old home. With all of this as a stumbling block, we will have to stay here until the leaves start piling up under the dining room table.

Selling your old house may take time because its appeal is limited to those with imagination, endurance and muted panache. Old-house lovers are in the minority and unlike the hardy pioneers of frontier days, everyone is looking for a combination of ease plus charisma, an ideal hard to satisfy without compromise. And, as one woman said after seeing our home and while shrewdly eyeing my husband, "I think it must take a unique type of person to live in an old house!"

"a unique type of person?"

Epilogue

I FEEL a compulsion to bring you up to date on a few details. My husband and one of our sons scaled the north face of our house and installed zigzag wires along some edges of the various roof levels. They finished just as winter closed in, congratulating themselves on a timely job, and it never snowed more than a dozen flakes all winter.

Last summer I worked on some of the unfinished painting inside that had been a hangover from five years before, but even that exertion left as many more areas incomplete. I am hoping to regain the initiative to try again soon. The blinds are still on the house, getting shabbier daily. I have consulted my friends about how they would feel if I removed them and to a person they say they love blinds. My quandary remains. Probably the most distressing development is that even as I write this update, I am under orders to pack up my sewing room for a move upstairs to the little room with its restored ceiling. My husband has run out of space and has progressed from mental measurements to physical ones.

We had our driveway resurfaced. A cover of "crush run" was decided upon; stones mixed with an ambiguous binder laid down over the regraded expanse. Unfortunately, the following day it started to rain and continued for a week, so most of the binder slid off toward the back yard leaving us scarcely better off than we were before.

Night noises have continued in the same desultory, unimaginative strain. One evening as I sat alone in the kitchen while a brisk wind whistled around the house outside, my thoughts were rudely interrupted by a loud crash in the cellar. I was unwilling to investigate, but felt, nonetheless, it would be irresponsible not to. After a perusal of the shadowy deep, I was unable to detect anything amiss and continued my search around the rest of the house. Surprised that everything looked as it should, I took another turn about the cellar and found that a Lally column had been dislodged and was lying prone on the floor. I was relieved, although hardly satisfied that it could produce such a blatant disturbance.

I have not found out what an electrician looks like yet, but a man came and took off some clapboards around the rotten post out front. He discovered that the damage (now positively identified as powderpost beetle mayhem) encompassed not only the post, but the front girt as well, one of the beams that is supposed to support my bedroom. Also he uncovered other friable timber in the rear of the house. It took him all day to find this double-barreled affliction and when he was done, he carefully spread both elevations with black tarpaper and has not been seen since. If he was discouraged, imagine how we feel? This is definitive proof that it seldom pays to go against one's better judgment and we are all advised to let well enough alone. The exterminator was fired.

And, finally, you should know that sex is still alive and thriving in the old house and there is reason to believe that worthwhile traditions, once firmly established, die hard.